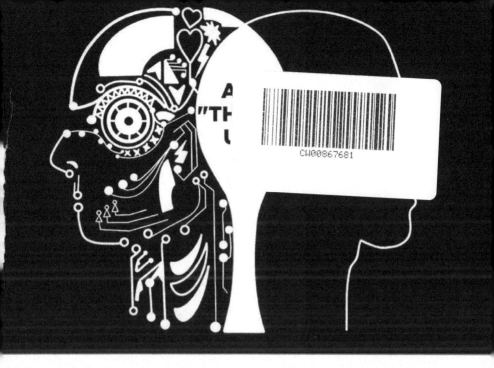

A SEMIOTIC VIEW OF MIXED IRON-CLAY FEET FROM DANIEL 2 IN THE AGE OF ARTIFICIAL INTELLIGENT TECHNOLOGY

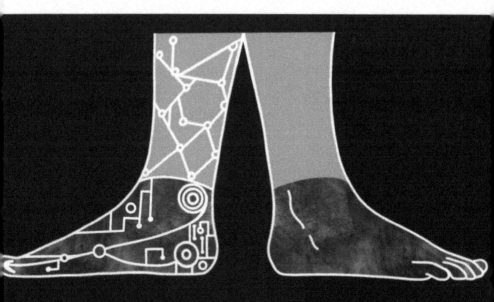

HOA HUU NGUYEN

GEORGE FOX UNIVERSITY

ARE "*THESE*" US?

A SEMIOTIC VIEW OF MIXED IRON-CLAY FEET

FROM DANIEL 2

IN THE AGE OF ARTIFICAL INTELLIGENT

TECHNOLOGY

A DISSERTATION SUBMITTED TO

THE FACULTY OF PORTLAND SEMINARY

IN CANDIDACY FOR THE DEGREE OF

DOCTOR OF MINISTRY

BY

HOA HUU NGUYEN

PORTLAND, OREGON

FEBRUARY 2020

Portland Seminary
George Fox University
Portland, Oregon
CERTIFICATE OF APPROVAL

_____

DMin Dissertation

_____

This is to certify that the DMin Dissertation of

Hoa Huu Nguyen
has been approved by
the Dissertation Committee
on February 21, 2020
for the degree of
Doctor of Ministry in Semiotics and Future Studies

Dissertation Committee:

Primary Advisor: Ron Clark, DMin
Secondary Advisor: Karen Claassen, DMin
Lead Mentor: Leonard I. Sweet, PhD

Xulon Press
2301 Lucien Way #415
Maitland, FL 32751
407.339.4217
www.xulonpress.com

Paperback ISBN-13: 978-1-6628-3385-4
eBook ISBN-13: 978-1-6628-3386-1

DEDICATION

TO THE LORD, THE CREATOR OF MY LIFE,

MY HEAVENLY FATHER.

TO MY WIFE, THE LOVER OF MY LIFE,

MY EARTHLY PARTNER.

ACKNOWLEDGMENTS

I would like to express my gratitude to the Lord, who has given me the strength and thoughtful knowledge to finish my Christian educational journey.

I would not have been able to finish this dissertation and my Doctor of Ministry without my wife, Thanh-Hoa Nguyen, who is not only my beloved wife but also my best friend and my earthly faithful praying partner. I will always be grateful for your love and your friendship.

Furthermore, I would like to thank my academic advisor Ron Clark, who has not only encouraged me to move on with this thesis but also led me all the way to the finish line with his intelligent mind and kind heart.

It would have been impossible for me to have achieved the new perspectives I did in interpreting this Biblical metaphor without the inspired mentorship of Dr. Leonard Sweet. I hope this dissertation shows how much I appreciate and treasure the remarkable insights he has taught me during my coursework in the Semiotics and Future Studies program these last few years. I will always be thankful to you Dr. Sweet.

I would like to thank Dr. Lori Wagner, my insightful and skilled editor, who has given my thesis a more fluent written style during her extremely tight schedule. I also thank George Fox Academy Writing Center for their help in proofreading several of my term papers, George Fox Daily Bruin for help conducting my Human-AI Culture Survey online to gather valuable survey responses, and George Fox Library for providing me hundreds of good books and online resources. Without the contributions of these departments, this research paper would never have been completed successfully.

I could not forget to thank my George Fox DMin Staff and Prayer Network, who encouraged me and prayed for me throughout this whole process. It made me feel safe to have them with me on my path of education in a foreign culture.

Finally, I thank my family members and the many friends from my Christian church community, who have supported me and prayed for me during my full-time job and full-time study.

My educational, physical, and spiritual journey would never be as blessed without all of you. You are my community of faith.

Table of Contents

PREFACE

Recently, hi-tech companies like Facebook, Google, Intel, Microsoft, IBM, and Hansen Robotics are taking on Artificial Intelligence (AI).[1] Creating humanoid-AI robots has become a hot controversy in our world today. In the next 30 years, imagine living in a potentially mixed Human-AI culture.[2] Human beings cohabitating with humanoid-AI robots may become reality in our daily life. The world as we know it may no longer be a purely human community but potentially a blended culture of humanity and humanoid-AI technology.

The world may soon be more and more populated by humanoid-AI beings!!! At that point, people may wonder:

Are *"These"* Us???

What differentiates us humans from our fellow humanoid-AI neighbors? Should we treat our humanoid-AI neighbors with the same rights and respect that we treat fellow humans? What are the dangers of allowing humanoid-AI partners and colleagues to make decisions with us, to be in relationship with us? What happens to our world as the lines between human and humanoid AI start to blur? How can or should the Church address these new dynamics already affecting our culture? As the humanoid-AI population grows, how will we change?

---

[1] AI: Artificial Intelligence.

[2] Human-AI culture: A mixed cuture between real human beings and humanoid-AI robots.

To begin to answer or even to ponder these questions as citizens of the world and ministers of the Church, we first need to remember our creation story. Why do I use the word *"these"* and not *"they"*? Because we humans are the creators of *these* beings. *"These"* beings did not and could not create us. *We human beings* are *the subjects, the creators,* of humanoid-AI beings. *Humanoid-AI beings* are the *objects/creatures* of a creator humanity.

The title—*Are "These" Us?*—may surprise the reader with what sounds like a strange grammatical anomaly, but its aim is to inform and remind readers that humanoid-AI beings can never be equal to human beings. No matter what intelligent algorithms Neural AI Networks have programmed into these beings by scientific innovators and AI technological developers, *these*—humanoid-AI creatures—will still remain a mere *creation* in the image of but not consistent with humanity, a brilliant but soulless set of inorganic beings that attest to a very human spirit and imagination.

To explore this dichotomy between creator and creation, this dissertation will investigate the biblical prophet Daniel's interpretation of the mixed iron-clay feet metaphor from Nebuchadnezzar's dream. This distinct biblical metaphor can provide for us today an important semiotic view of what a potentially mixed culture of human beings and humanoid-AI robots in the age of AI technology and cyborgs might look like, and what it might mean for us and for our future in society and in the Church.

ABSTRACT

This research offers a semiotic application of Daniel's prophetic *'mixed iron and clay feet'* interpretation from Nebuchadnezzar's dream. This prophecy may be used to predict a potentially mixed Human-AI culture and its impacts on Christian faith in the age of AI and cyborgs. The Christian faith traditionally has not applied Daniel's iron-clay feet metaphor to a potentially mixed Human-AI reality. However, I will argue that by employing this semiotic interpretation, we can inform and guide Christ's Church, which continues to remain grossly unprepared for the questions and challenges raised by a burgeoning Human-AI culture. Knowledge of this topic will prepare the church better to navigate its future.

In a potentially blended Human-AI culture, a significant opportunity exists for the Church to define what it means to be fully human and to provide a redemptive, ethical, and theological framework for the benefit of humanity in the new AI technological age. This dissertation suggests how effective Christian faith can be communicated to a blended Human-AI culture with openness, with loving mission, and maintaining the belief that God—the Alpha and the Omega—is always in control no matter how advanced our technology gets.

Chapter 1 presents a semiotic analysis of the metallic human statue from Nebuchadnezzar's dream through Daniel's interpretation in Dan. 2. This leads the reader into a historical journey through the earthly kingdoms represented by the different metallic portions in that human statue—the gold head, the silver chest and arms, the bronze belly and thigh, the iron legs, and the mixed iron-clay feet.

Chapter 2 provides 1) an overview of Biblical scholars' interpretations of the mixed iron-clay feet metaphor through the historical lens of humanity and 2) a view of the metaphor as a potentially mixed culture between humans and humanoid AI beings, as seen through my own semiotic lens. I will explain why I chose the clay metaphor for human beings and the iron metaphor for humanoid-AI beings and will suggest how this metaphor can be helpful to us today in contemplating our own current and future culture.

Chapter 3 discusses the traditional Christian belief in God's creation and the rise of humanoid-AI beings through the two most applicable stories controversially debated in our time—the story of the Garden of Eden and the story of the computer lab. This chapter supports my traditional Christian belief in the image of God, the matter of flesh, and the matter of the soul in responding to the question of *'what does it mean to be fully human in the mixed Human-AI culture?'*

Chapter 4 further explores the analysis of what it means to be fully human and asks how the ethical framework, the redemptive framework, and the theological framework of Christianity's rethinking effectively might work in a mixed Humanoid-AI culture.

Chapter 5 suggests how Christians can turn cultural challenges into opportunities in order to communicate Christian faith and the gospel with openness and with loving kindness by affirming what it means to be human in responding to the question 'Are *"These"* Us?' The chapter will also affirm our faith in an Alpha and Omega God, who is always in control no matter what will happen in a future full of mysteries and brokenness.

Chapter 6 will conclude with insights into what I have learned from both science and Christianity that could help us affirm the humanness of humanity in the midst of a potentially mixed Human-AI culture. This chapter will be an open invitation for people to continue discussion into this important area of research and will invite people within the Church today to seek answers for themselves not through human political power, nor through scientific and technological supper intelligence, but through the only Person—the Son of Man and the Son of God—"Jesus Christ is the same yesterday and today and forever" (Heb. 13:8 NRSV).[3]

---

[3] NRSV: New Revised Standard Version of the Bible, copyright © 1989 Division of Christian Education of the National Council of the Churches of Christ in the USA. Used by permission. All rights reserved. All future references in this dissertation, unless indicated, will appear in NRSV translation.

CHAPTER 1:
AN ANALYSIS OF NEBUCHANEZZAR'S
DREAM IN DANIEL 2

In the beginning God dreamed a new creation, one that would emerge from the chaos of a formless darkness. This new creation in God's mind would be a great planet inhabited with colorful and plentiful living creatures. The king of darkness could never imagine that the Almighty God could create an amazing technology that would dispel the power of darkness, break through the shadows of death, and teem with life. This primal technology I call the First Technology of Light. This First Technology of Light connected God's dream with a new and living world of creation that marked the beginning of time.

Dreams are important, because they can create new images for us of the world. They promote a mentality that can enable us to move into a new level of life, in which they just might make the impossible possible. Through God's power of dream, the First Technology of Light was generated, God's creation came into existence, and human beings were created in the image of God to fulfill the desire of God's heart. Through a dream, the fate of humanity was revealed, the mystery of a future was unlocked, and a new technology came into being. Christian World News (CBN) stated: "Dreams are one of the most overlooked forms of communication used by God. The Word of God consistently reveals God as speaking to people through this universally experienced and mysterious phenomenon."[1]

Nebuchadnezzar's dream was one of the most phenomenal dreams in the Bible interpreted by the prophet Daniel during the Judahites' captivity in the Babylonian kingdom. I chose to exegete this dream in this dissertation, because this message from God reveals a phenomenon of divine-human technology, represented in the metallic human statue from Nebuchadnezzar's dream—from the gold head to the silver chest and arms, to the bronze belly and thigh, to the iron legs, and then to the mixed iron-clay feet. The mixed iron-clay feet metaphor is the main focus of my thesis, as it is my semiotic application to a potentially mixed culture between human beings and humanoid-AI robots (Human-AI culture) in the age of AI technology and cyborgs.

The metallic forms of the statue change from the most to the least value to denote that human value has been decayed through technology from ancient times to the present time. The more sophisticated human technology becomes, the more civilized the human world becomes, and the worse humanity becomes separated from God and isolated from other human beings.

As AI technology continues to rapidly advance in our time, humanoid-AI robots may be mass-produced. At that time, a humanoid-AI robot may be recognized as a citizen of a nation in the human world, and the borderline between humanity and humanoid AI will become thinner. Because

---

[1] Bryan Carraway, "A Theological Look at Spiritual Dreams," *CBN*, accessed February 12, 2020, https://www1.cbn.com/theological-look-spiritual-dreams.

humanoid-AI robots will be created in human-like form with an AI 'brain' programmed with super-intelligent algorithms, they might be considered intellectually to be on the same level as humans. Thus, a potentially mixed Human-AI culture could come into existence in the near future, along with a wave of controversial debates that span next couple of decades.

If the dream of God's heart is fulfilled by the image of God in humanity, perhaps the dream of a human's heart is to have the image of a human present in a humanoid-AI machine. Semiotically, the mixed iron-clay feet metaphor interpreted in Daniel 2, may point to a coming reality as our age of AI technology advances in the future to come.

God works and controls everything in God's own time and reveals mysteries to God's loving children in their greatest times of weariness and brokenness; and that repeats throughout human history. One of the greatest stories of the ancient times was Daniel's interpretation of a metallic statue from Nebuchadnezzar's dream, in which God rolled up a Judahite mystery curtain to reveal the future of humanity (Dan. 2:28-35 NRSV).

Being a captive in a foreign land, a noble Judahite young man was lifted up by God, chosen to be trained in the Babylonian kingdom, and placed in the Babylonian king's palace. Yet Daniel's intelligence would not help him escape the miseries of a brutal death penalty unless he could unlock for powerful, dictatorial King Nebuchadnezzar the mysteries of the future, as relayed by God within his dreams. Yahweh's intervention to protect the lives of the children of Judah would reveal to the Babylonian emperor that the Lord God

YHWH is the Ruler of everyone and controls the flourishing or falling of every earthly kingdom.

Nebuchadnezzar did not know that the name of Babylon had been recorded in the Lord's book thousands of years before he came into being. The Lord had dealt prior with an ancient Babylonian ruler and had left his arrogance as a mark of human failure. Similarly, Yahweh now would deal with Nebuchadnezzar and his Babylonian kingdom in a way that would make this king recognize Yahweh as All Sovereign God.

For many millennia, human history has shifted power from one kingdom to another. During this time, God would raise one kingdom and overthrow another to maintain justice in the world's power. Kingdoms began in ancient times, after the Fall of Humanity, as Adam's descendants began to establish their own rulers, to build cities to reserve their territories from other tribes, and to build walls to protect themselves from wild animals or other enemies.

The first city mentioned in the Bible was the city of Enoch, which was named after Cain's son (Gen. 4:17 NRSV). This city was built by Cain after he killed his own brother, Abel. After the flood in Noah's time, the first ancient kingdom in the Bible was established by Ham—the father of Canaan, Noah's cursed son, who "saw the nakedness of his father and told his two brothers outside" (Gen. 9:22 NRSV). Perhaps, the curse from Noah had given Ham some feeling of failure and abandon. However, Ham's descendant, a grandson, Nimrod, who grew to become "a mighty warrior" on the earth, became the first ruler recorded in the Bible, who built his own kingdom (Babylon) beyond his grandfather's curses (Gen. 10:8-10 NIV)[2]. Nimrod's life was to prove that he could become the man who firmly stood in God's presence. Even without his ancestor's blessings, Nimrod would be a great man, because God was with him, and God is stronger than those in this world. Genesis 10 reveals God's mercy through a story of Nimrod, in which the representative of an abandoned generation had become an abundant generation before the Lord:

> He was a mighty hunter before the Lord; that is why it is said, "Like Nimrod, a mighty hunter before the Lord. The first centers of his kingdom were Babylon, Uruk, Akkad, and Kalneh in Shinar. From that land he went to Assyria where he built Nineveh, Rehoboth Ir, Calah and Resen, which is between Nineveh and Calah; that is the great city" (Gen. 10:9-11 NIV).

However, the name of Nimrod seems to have had a negative meaning that is opposite to the positive image of *a mighty warrior before the Lord* described in Genesis 10. According to professor Ronald S. Hendel:

> Nimrod (literally, "we will rebel" or "let us rebel" in Hebrew) is described in Genesis 10:8-12 as a mighty hunter before Yahweh. . . Nimrod's name is likely a polemical distortion of the name of the Mesopotamian god Ninurta, who was a mighty hunter and warrior, a culture hero, and in some text the ruler of the universe. . . In postbiblical traditions,

---

[2] New International Version (NIV), Holy Bible, New International Version®, NIV® Copyright ©1973, 1978, 1984, 2011 by Biblica Inc.® Used by permission. All rights reserved worldwide.

Nimrod, the inciter of "rebellion" who ruled Babel, was often identified as a giant and as the chief builder of the tower of Babel.[3]

For the Hebrew people, Nebuchadnezzar's Babylon would always be a reminder of Nimrod's tower of Babel. David Burke indicates: "Babel is the Hebrew word for Babylon, which the Babylonian themselves explained as meaning "the gate of God" . . . The meaning is significant for a famous city whose central temple tower was said to reach the heavens."[4]

At Babel, Yahweh's sovereignty was proven over humans by the metaphor of languages which God used to confuse their tongues. As a result, people could not understand each other, their strength was broken, and they stopped their acts of arrogance in reaching to the heavens.

The Babylonians' renowned technology of brick architecture became for us a symbol of human imperfection and brokenness. For the first time in the history of humanity, at the Tower of Babel—*the gate of God*, a symbol of an ancient Babylon—the Almighty Creator proved that human history is His Story, that God is Creator of and above human beings. Thus, the Lord is in control no matter what humans do, no matter what their efforts to reject the will of God.

Another time in human history during the exile of the Judahites in Babylon—again at the *gate of God*—God

---

[3] Bruce M. Metzger and Michael D. Coogan, eds., *The Oxford Guide to People and Places of the Bible* (New York: Oxford University Press, 2001), 218.

[4] Bruce M. Metzger and Michael D. Coogan, eds., 28.

revealed God's sovereignty over humans through the metaphor of a metallic human figure from Nebuchadnezzar's dream in which the prophet Daniel interpreted that human glory would be decayed from the best value to the least as they grew stronger in power. At the end, human power and all earthly kingdoms together with their advanced technologies and their best modern civilizations would be crushed down by a mere humble rock from heaven (Dan. 2:28-35 NRSV). The destruction of the metallic human figure signified the reality of human weakness and helplessness when facing the Alpha and Omega God—the One Above All Things, beyond Heaven, Earth, and the deepest depths of Hell.

Is there a certain coincidence between Nimrod, Noah's unselected descendant, the ruler of the old Babylon in ancient times, and Nebuchadnezzar, a pagan king, the ruler of new Babylon in Daniel's time? Would it be possible that Daniel's prophetic interpretation of Nebuchadnezzar's dream is another way to retell the story of human kingdoms and to recite an emphasis of God's authority throughout human history?

This dissertation asserts that human kingdoms are represented by the gold head, the silver arms and chest, the bronze belly and thigh, the iron legs, and the mixed iron-clay feet in the statue from Nebuchadnezzar's dream. It also addresses biblical scholars' different interpretations of these kingdoms in human history before the rock cut out of a mountain—not by human hands—smashes all worldly kingdoms and becomes the everlasting kingdom of the Sovereign God. Furthermore, this dissertation suggests a new semiotic view of the mixed iron-clay feet metaphor as a potentially mixed culture between humans and humanoid artificial intelligent robots (Human-AI culture) in the advanced technology age of artificial intelligence (AI). This dissertation promotes some ideas about a potentially mixed Human-AI culture in the near future and how the church could be prepared to deal with questions and challenges about ethics and behaviors, personhood, and the matter of the soul. The church must continue God's calling mission to prepare the next Christian generations, who will positively live within a potentially mixed Human-AI culture, and must learn to communicate the Christian faith positively in the age of AI and cyborgs.

Gold Head

Nebuchadnezzar's dream was a reminder that God holds the future, and God had revealed the mystery of the future to the Babylonian king who was seeking the answer of the time to come (Dan. 2:29 NRSV). Nebuchadnezzar had failed to see that Yahweh of Judah had given him permission to rule, and he had become arrogant. However, God granted Nebuchadnezzar "the kingdom, the power, the might, and the glory" (Dan. 2:37-38 NRSV) and made him the greatest king of his time. Carol Newsom wrote that God placed Nebuchadnezzar as the ruler over his kingdom as Nebuchadnezzar placed Daniel to care for his Babylonian kingdom.[5] It was amazing that Nebuchadnezzar entrusted

---

[5] Carol A. Newsom, *Daniel: The Old Testament Library* (Louisville, KY: Westminster John Knox Press, 2014), 74-75.

Daniel—a slave—with the top position in the Babylonian political ladder after only one interview with Daniel, and he gave Daniel a new identity regardless of who and what Daniel was before. As a result, king Nebuchadnezzar would raise a high bar before the Lord since Nebuchadnezzar was far from having a conservative and prejudiced way of thinking. He was an admirable and decent king, who deserved a new title *golden head* from the Lord.

Many scholars suggest that Daniel's interpretation of Nebuchadnezzar as a gold head was true since he built a huge gold statue as an idol for people to worship, and gold was plentiful in his kingdom.[6] In addition, scholar Stephen Leston noted that in Nebuchadnezzar's time, Babylon was the most glorious kingdom on Earth, and "the garden of Babylon was one of the wonders of the ancient world."[7] Nebuchadnezzar grew in power, and his kingdom expanded throughout many nations on earth as Daniel described: "Your Majesty, . . . You have become great and strong; your greatness has grown until it reaches the sky, and your

---

Nebuchadnezzar was not only a proud and arrogant monarch who ultimately came to understand and publicly acknowledge the supreme sovereignty of Israel's God but also was someone to whom God entrusted knowledge of the plan for the epochs of world history that Nebuchadnezzar later initiated.

[6] Robert Gurney, *God in Control* (Worthing West Sussex, England: H.E Walter, 1980), 30. See also Willian B. Nelson, *Daniel: Understanding the Bible Commentary Series* (Grand Rapids, MI: Baker Books, 2012), 90. See additionally Edward G. Dobson, *Daniel: Making the Right Choices* (Grand Rapids, MI: Baker Books, 1994), 49.

[7] Stephen Leston, *The Bible in World History: How History and Scripture Intersect* (Urichsville, OH: Barbour Books, 2011), 147.

dominion extends to distant parts of the earth" (Dan. 4:22 NIV).

However, the metallic human statue in Nebuchadnezzar's dream signaled a warning from the Almighty God that all earthly kingdoms were metallic pieces of the whole, decaying in value, being easily broken, easily falling apart, and temporary. Babylon would not be an exception and its days were also numbered. Lynn Arner comments on the change of kingship as a historical film footage. If movie footage has an ending period, similarly, an earthly kingdom also declines and collapses in its cycle.

> The structure of Nebuchadnezzar's statue forms a teleological history. The age of gold becomes the age of silver; the age of silver leads into the epoch of brass; the epoch of brass turns into the era of iron; and the era of iron ends in the days of iron and clay. History begins with a golden age and gradually proceeds in a linear movement through progressively lower levels of being, indicated by the association of each successive epoch with an increasingly less valuable metal.[8]

As the statue pieces were temporary, so the glory of the Babylonian kingdom would fade away as well.[9] How did the Babylonian kingdom fall? God did not let Babylon fall during the reign of king Nebuchadnezzar, since he

---

[8] Lynn Arner, "History Lesson from the End of Time: Gower and the English Rising of 1381," *Clio* 31, no. 3 (2002): 242, ProQuest.

[9] Oliver B.Greene, *Daniel: Verse by Verse Study* (Greenville, SC: Gospel House, 1964), 87-88.

acknowledged God and glorified God after God had warned him of his arrogance in his second dream—the big tree that was chopped down to the ground. That dream was a sign from God for him that he would be driven away from humans to eat the herbs of the field as the oxen did until he would honor the most-high God who rules over human kingdoms, who had the right to recover him and to restore his kingdom (Dan. 4:10-16 NRSV).

Babylon fell instead during the reign of Nebuchadnezzar's descendant, King Belshazzar, who celebrated a wine festival with a thousand of his nobles, his wives, and his concubines. While they were drinking wine using the gold goblets that had been taken from the temple of God in Jerusalem and praising their idol gods, that same evening, a hand from God wrote on the wall the warning words to prophesy the end of the Babylonian kingdom. Daniel in Dan. 5:18-31 (NRSV) explained God's decision to Belshazzar and interpreted God's warning.

The fall of Babylon was very fast during the night of king Belshazzar's wine festival. According to scholar Edward Young, when Cyrus approached Babylon, the Babylonians retreated to Babylon city. Cyrus had to lead his army to the Euphrates, crossing the shallow river channel that led to Babylon city following the path prepared by Gobryas in order to capture Babylon that same night without a fight.[10] John Whitcomb claims, "Babylon fell on the

---

[10] Edward J. Young, *The Prophecy of Daniel: A Commentary* (Philadelphia, PA: WM. B. Eerdmans Publishing, 1972), 128. See also John J. Collins, *Daniel: Hermeneia—A Critical and Historical*

sixteenth day of Tishri (Oct.11/12, 539 BCE) as indicated in the Nabonidus Chronicle." [11]

Silver Chest and Arms

Daniel explained to Nebuchadnezzar that "after you shall arise another kingdom inferior to yours" (Dan. 2:39 NRSV). Persia was the next kingdom represented as the Silver Chest and Arms. It's interesting to know that "taxes were paid in silver in Medo-Persia." [12] Persia was not stronger than Babylon,[13] but the Persians and Medes would arise and later overthrow the Babylonian kingdom under Belshazzar (Dan 5:30-31 NRSV). Isaiah had prophesized this transition of power from Babylon to the Persian king Cyrus. He too was left, by Yahweh, in charge of the kingdom.

> Who says of Cyrus, "He is my shepherd, and he shall carry out all my purpose"; and who says of Jerusalem, "It shall be rebuilt," and of the temple, "Your foundation shall be laid." Thus says

Commentary on the Bible (Minneapolis, MN: Fortress Press, 1993), 252-253.

[11] John C. Whitcomb, *Darius the Mede: A Study in History Identification* (Grand Rapids, MI: Eerdmans, 1959),73.

[12] Sign of the End Times: "The Prophecy of Daniel 2," http://www.signs-of-end-times.com/daniel-2-prophecy.html.

[13] Green, *Daniel: Verse by Verse Study*, 88. History reveals that this kingdom was Persia. . . Silver is inferior to gold; and the head of gold, most powerful of all, was follow by silver—A little weaker, a little less powerful. . . The Media-Persia Empire was inferior to Babylon in wealth, in luxury, and in magnificence.

the LORD to his anointed, to Cyrus, whose right hand I have grasped to subdue nations before him and strip kings of their robes, to open doors before him—and the gates shall not be closed: I will go before you and level the mountains, I will break in pieces the doors of bronze and cut through the bars of iron, I will give you the treasures of darkness and riches hidden in secret places, so that you may know that it is I, the LORD, the God of Israel, who call you by your name. For the sake of my servant Jacob, and Israel my chosen, I call you by your name, I surname you, though you do not know me (Isa. 44:28, 45:1-4 NRSV).

Greene also comments:

Cyrus was foreordained over a hundred years before his birth to do two things as ordered by God Almighty. . . The first thing that he would do was to conquer Babylon . . . The second thing . . . was to issue an edict at the close of the Babylonian captivity, giving the Jews the right to return to Jerusalem and rebuild their temple. This edict was given by Cyrus in 536 B. C.[14]

It seems like God's sovereignty is repeated over and over again in human history. Any pagan king who has an open-hearted and open-minded lifestyle would be a useful tool in God's hand to enforce justice on earth and bring peace for God's chosen people. In the Babylonian kingdom, God enthroned king Nebuchadnezzar, but God overthrew evil

---

[14] Greene, *Daniel: Verse by Verse Study*, 90-91. When Cyrus took Babylon in 538 B. C., his uncle, Darius, was king of Media.

king Belshazzar and ended the reign of the Babylonian empire in human history. The Persian ruler Cyrus had been prepared by God, a century before he came into being, for good purposes—to redeem Yahweh's chosen people, to rebuild Yahweh's temple, and to fulfil Yahweh's promises at the appointed time of the Lord.

Xenophon notes that "Cyrus was most handsome of person, most generous of heart, most devoted to learning, and most ambitious, so that he endured all sorts of labor and faced all sorts of danger."[15] Cyrus took the throne of Persia in 558 BCE; in 553 BCE he struck the first battle with the Media empire and conquered Media around 550 BCE. His empire then included both the Medes and Persians, and it became the Medo-Persian empire.[16]

According to John Whitcomb, in 530 BCE Cyrus left the throne to his son, Cambyses. While Cambyses was titled the "King of Babylon," Cyrus retained the title "King of Lands," as his ambition was to conquer more nations in the northeast. Far from home, Cyrus died on the battlefield in the autumn of the same year. His son Cambyses ruled the Persian Empire.[17]

Instead of having new kingdoms raised up after the fall of Babylon as Daniel interpreted, Collins suggests that the four metallic pieces of the statue represent the four kings

---

[15] Don Nardo, *World History Series: The Persian Empire* (San Diego, CA: Lucent Books, 1998), 36.

[16] Don Nardo, 26-27.

[17] John C. Whitcomb, *Darius the Mede*, 71.

of Babylon—Nebuchadnezzar, Amelmarduk, Neriglissar, and Nabonidus—rather than four separated kingdoms.[18] Regardless of the interpretation, it seems clear that Cyrus played an important role in the dream. Cyrus and Medo-Persia would last until today if there had not been a third kingdom as Daniel interpreted. Thus, Green's commentary seems fitting into the context of Daniel's interpretation more than Collins' view.

Finally, the Persian Empire fell into the hands of Alexander the Great. Green also notes: "In 331 BCE Alexander the Grecian conquered Media-Persia, and the third world empire came into being."[19]

Bronze Belly and Thigh

Daniel prophesied about "a third kingdom of bronze, which shall rule over the whole earth" (Dan 2:39 NRSV). "An interesting note concerning the kingdom of Greece, . . . is that their soldiers wore armor made of *Bronze*. This obviously matches the brass thighs of the image. So, we can see that the future kingdoms not only matched the figure of a man, but the metals used also."[20]

Alexander the Great was the king of Greece. He became a legendary king, because he "conquered more nations at the fastest rate than any other ancient king. In

---

[18] John Collins J., *Daniel: A Commentary on the Book of Daniel* (Minneapolis, MN: Fortress Press, 1993), 168.

[19] Greene, Daniel: Verse by Verse Study, 91.

[20] Sign of the End Time, "The Prophecy of Daniel 2."

thirteen years, he gained control of the entire Mediterranean world, much of North Africa, Mesopotamia, and extended his reach as far as India—never losing a battle."[21]

Robin Lane Fox exemplifies Alexander's heroic brave characters:

> Most historians have had their own Alexander, and a view of him which in one-sided is bound to have missed the truth. There are features which cannot be disputed; the extraordinary toughness of a man who sustained nine wounds, breaking an ankle bone and receiving an arrow through his chest and the bolt of a catapult through his shoulder. He was twice struck on the head and neck by stones and once lost his sight from such a blow. The bravery which bordered on folly never failed him in the front line of battle, a position which few generals since have considered proper; he set out to show himself a hero, and from the Granicus to Multan he left a trail of heroics which has never been surpassed and is perhaps too easily assumed among all his achievements.[22]

Tony Spawforth commends the ruler: "the short-lived reign of Alexander –thirteen years – was, as one Roman historian wrote much later, 'a brilliant flash of

---

[21] Jeremiah David, Agents of Babylon: What the Prophet Daniel Tells Us about the End of Days (Carol Stream, IL: Tyndale House, 2015), 210.

[22] Robin Lane Fox, *Alexander the Great* (New York, NY: Penguin Books, 2004), 495-496.

lighting.'"[23] Finally, the ambition of the great conqueror—Alexander the Great—ended in sickness. Greene indicates that Alexander the Great died at a young age of thirty-three in 323 BCE. Then, his kingdom was divided in to four kingdoms: Thrace, Macedonia, Syria and Egypt.[24]

According to Martin, after the death of Alexander the Great, his generals who had no blood relationship with Alexander, took over his kingdom, made themselves kings, and founded the Hellenistic kingdoms.[25] Spawforth views the Greek world behind Alexander's death as the *Game of Thrones.*' He adds: "Alexander's failures to secure the hereditary succession lay at the heart of this drama. His vulnerable widow and posthumous son, as well as the half-brother with a mental disorder who briefly succeeded him, were all slaughtered."[26]

Martin discovered that during Hellenistic times, the Hebrew Bible was translated into Greek. He also noticed that the Hellenistic Jews, who were living among Hellenistic communities, refused to worship Greek idols. A remarkable event in the Hellenistic world was the Jewish movement called the *Maccabean Revolt.* This Revolt was led by Judah, the famous Jewish leader who took back Jerusalem temple

---

[23] Tony Spawforth, *The Story of Greece and Rome* (New Haven, CT: Yale University Press, 2018), 168.

[24] Green, Daniel: Verse by Verse Study, 91-92.

[25] Thomas R. Martin, *Ancient Greek: From Prehistoric to Hellenistic Times* (New Haven and London: Yale University Press, 2013), 199.

[26] Spawforth, The Story of Greece and Rome, 177, 179.

for the devotion to the worship of Jewish Yahweh during the reign of the Seleucid king Antiochus IV, a pagan king who prohibited the Jews to practice their religious rituals. He converted the Jewish temple into a temple for the Syrian god, Baal Shamen. The Maccabean Revolt was a remarkable victory that earned Jewish independence. As a result, Hellenistic Jews celebrated their Hanukkah holiday after twenty-five years of fighting with the Seleucids.[27]

History proved that Greece under Antiochus—one of Alexander's generals who became an evil king claiming to be a god—severely persecuted the Jews because they refused to worship his idols. Antiochus also violated the Jerusalem Temple. Finally, he died through a horrible disease.[28] It seemed that God had intervened in human history and brought justice to God's people. "By now, Greekness had long ceased to be a monopoly of ethnic Greeks. It had become a marker of a type of cultural civilization attractive to non-Greeks as well. As it turned out later, the Romans would be by far the most significant of the non-Greek peoples who succumbed to the allure of Greek cultural achievement."[29]

---

[27] Martin, *Ancient Greek*, 220.

[28] David, *Agent of Babylon*, 245-246. Antiochus professed to be God himself. The coins minted during his reign bore these words: *Antiochus, Theos Epiphanes*, meaning, "Antiochus, God Manifest." See also James L. Kugel, *How to Read the Bible: A guide to Scripture, Then and Now* (New York, NY: Free Press, 2017), 651-652.

[29] Spawforth, 192.

Iron Legs

Daniel described, "There shall be a fourth kingdom, strong as iron; just as iron crushes and smashes everything, it shall crush and shatter all these" (Dan 2:40 NRSV).

In the ancient wars, iron was one of the strongest metals and most lethal weapons. This fourth kingdom represented a fearful government and its military power that would quickly defeat any adversary. Some scholars debate that the fourth kingdom is not to be the Roman Empire, but Greece. However, others agree that the Roman Empire would be the kingdom of *iron legs* since iron weapons were used in its army.[30]

John Gill agrees with other scholars about Rome's cruel power not only to the Jews but also to other nations in all the world.[31] Joseph Benson has similar thoughts of Roman Empire and describes Rome as the strongest empire

---

[30] Sign of the End Time, "The Prophecy of Daniel 2." Iron was widely used in the armor and weapons of the Roman Empire. This was probably the least 'glorious' kingdom, but certainly the strongest, as Rome was known for its so called 'iron grip' during its reign. See also Arthur E. Bloomfield, *The End of the Days* (Minneapolis, MN: Bethany Fellowship Press, 1961), 91. The fourth kingdom was the Roman Empire, which ruled the world with an iron hand. It destroyed Jerusalem in 70 A.D. and completed the dispersion of the Jews. See additionally Greene, *Daniel: Verse by Verse Study*, 94.

[31] Bible Hub, "Daniel 2: Gill's Exposition," accessed July 8, 2019, https://biblehub.com/commentaries/gill/daniel/2.htm. The fourth kingdom shall be strong as iron, . . . the Roman empire is compared to iron for its strength, firmness, and duration in itself; and for its power over other nations; and also for its cruelty to the Jews above all others, in utterly destroying their city, temple, and nation.

compared to the previous three—the golden Babylon, the silver Persia, and the bronze Macedonia—and its two "Roman consults" are suitable to the metaphor of the two legs of iron in the statue.[32]

Green notes, "finally, the Roman Empire was divided into the Eastern and Western Empires. . . The two legs symbolize the two parts of the Roman Empire—the eastern division and the western division. Constantinople was the capital of the eastern division; Rome was the capital of the west."[33]

Daniel continues describing the fourth kingdom to Nebuchadnezzar:

> And there shall be a fourth kingdom, strong as iron; just as iron crushes and smashes everything, it shall crush and shatter all these. As you saw the feet and toes partly of potter's clay and partly of iron, it shall be a divided kingdom; but some of the strength of iron shall be in it, as you saw the iron mixed with the clay. As the toes of the feet were part iron and part clay, so the kingdom shall be partly strong and partly brittle. As you saw the iron mixed with clay, so will they mix with one another in marriage, but they will not hold together, just as iron does not mix with clay (Dan. 2:40-43 NRSV).

---

[32] Bible Hub, "Daniel 2: Benson's Commentary," accessed July 8, 2019, https://biblehub.com/commentaries/benson/daniel/2.htm.

[33] Greene, 94.

Mixed Iron-Clay Feet

Daniel's interpretation above clearly demonstrates that no earthy kingdom will rise as a successor of the fourth kingdom. This fourth kingdom will last but will be divided into smaller kingdoms—ten kingdoms—and they are half strong and half weak accordingly to the attributes of the iron and the clay in the mixed iron-clay feet.[34] Benson and others have similar views of the metaphor of the mixed kingdoms in which the kingdom will be divided between the strong and the weak people—these are the ten nations that rose against the Roman Empires, they went after different interests and political desires, and they mixed together but would not be united together. [35]

In contrast, Collins suggests that "the mixture of iron and clay is taken to refer to the shared power between Nabonidus and Belshazzar. This prophesy understood and predicted the fall of Babylon but may have been of either

---

[34] Sign of the End Time, "The Prophecy of Daniel 2." The Roman Empire as a one world power disintegrated due to the attacks from the barbarian tribes. By 476 AD Rome had lost its power and the tribes that sacked the Roman Empire became the 10 nations of Europe. These tribes were the Ostrogoth, Visigoths, Franks, Vandals, Alemannians, Sueves, Anglo-Saxons, Heruli, Lombards, and Burgundians.

[35] Bible Hub, "Benson's Commentary." As the toes of the feet were part of iron and part of clay, so the kingdom shall be partly strong and partly broken. . . The conjunction of the Romans with the conquered nations, and afterward with the Goths, Vandals, and other barbarians, who subverted the empire, seems to be here intended: in consequence of which these ten kingdoms became a medley of people, of different nations, laws, and customs. But they shall not cleave one to another.

Gentile or Jew origin.[36] Nelson adds a different view of the mixed iron-clay feet metaphor which represents the intermarriage between two royal families of the Seleucids and the Ptolemies. However, he believes this not to be a strong argument.[37]

A Stone from Heaven

From Daniel's interpretation, the fourth kingdom will be struck down, not by human power but by power outside the human realm—a stone from the God of Heaven. That stone will destroy all earthly kingdoms and will establish God's everlasting Kingdom over humanity in God's timing. Daniel prophesized the end of pagan kingdoms:

> In the days of those kings the God of heaven will set up a kingdom that shall never be destroyed, nor shall this kingdom be left to another people. It shall crush all these kingdoms and bring them to an end, and it shall stand forever; just as you saw that a stone was cut from the mountain not by hands, and that it crushed the iron, the bronze, the clay, the silver, and the gold. The great God has informed the king what shall be hereafter. The dream is certain, and its interpretation trustworthy (Dan. 2:44-45 NRSV).

---

[36] John Collins J., *Daniel*, 169.

[37] Nelson, *"Daniel,"* 91. A more literal rendering would be "they will be mixed with the seed of man," mixed families, mixed marriages, mixed offspring. As already mentioned, this probably refers to intermarriage between two royal families, the Seleucids and the Ptolemies.

Collins views the stone crushing all pagan kingdoms as the final destruction of all pagan idolatry and their ruling power.[38] Other scholars and the Jews see the stone fulfilled in the Jewish nation. However, most scholars agree that the stone cut out from the mountain not by hands may be *the Son of Man* as described in Dan. 7:13 (NIV), who also represents Jesus Christ later in the New Testament.[39]

Jesus took this stone title for himself as He said, "Have you never read in the scriptures: 'The stone that the builders rejected has become the cornerstone; this was the Lord's doing, and it is amazing in our eyes'? . . . The one who falls on this stone will be broken to pieces; and it will crush anyone on whom it falls" (Matt. 21:42, 44 NRSV). In addition, Jesus repeatedly called Himself *the Son of Man* during His time on earth (Matt. 8:20, 9:6, 10:23 NRSV). This confirmed Daniel's prophesy. The *Son of Man* (Dan. 7:13

---

[38] Collins, *Daniel*, 171. Another strand of Christian interpretation identified the stone as the church. . . From the viewpoint of the Jewish author, the gentile kingdoms constitute a unit, appropriately represented by the statue. While the statue is not an idol, it inevitably recalls idolatrous statues . . . What is destroyed here is gentile power and the idolatry it implies.

[39] John F. Walvoord, *Daniel: The Key to Prophet Revelation* (Chicago, IL: Moody Press, 1971), 168. Obviously, the expression *Son of Man* should be interpreted by the context. . . It corresponds clearly to the Scripture which predicts that Christ will rule over all nations (Ps. 72:11; Rev. 19:15-16). Only Christ will come with clouds of heaven and be King of kings and Lord of lords over all nations through eternity. See also Edward J. Young, *The Prophesy of Daniel*, 79. Most Christian expositors find the reference in Christ and the progress of His Kingdom, and this seems to me to be correct. The stone is represented as not being cut of the mountain by hands in order to show that it is prepared, not by men, but by God.

NIV) would be fulfilled in Jesus and completely fulfilled in the return of Jesus (Matt. 24:27, 30 NRSV), at the appointed time of God in the end time. Finally, "the kingdom of God will completely triumph, and the kingdom of men (as represented by the image) will be completely destroyed."[40]

CONCLUSION

From the time Daniel interpreted Nebuchadnezzar's dream until our present time, world history proved that Daniel's prophesy was not a legend but a reason for the success or the failure of worldly kingdoms. The metallic pieces of the whole statue that change from the most to the least valuable metal signified a warning that when the fear of God withered from human hearts, the fearfulness within human life increased.

One interpretation of world history suggests that the four kings represented in Daniel's interpretation were the Babylonian, Medes-Persian, Greek, and Roman Empire. As the metals in the statue were decaying in value but stronger than the previous ones, so too did the later kingdoms become more inferior to the former ones. "The first world empire was singular—one unit. The second empire was divided— dual Media-Persia. The third empire was quadruple—four generals ruled in four sections. The fourth empire in its final form will be a "ten-toed" kingdom."[41] However, all world power will be crushed by the stone from Heaven and all

---

[40] Edward J. Young, 79.

[41] Oliver B. Greene, Daniel: Verse by Verse Study, 94.

world rulers will end their terms. The stone symbolizes the *Son of Man*—Jesus Christ—the Lord of all lords and the King of all kings. He will establish God's Everlasting Kingdom in the end time, and God will reign forever with God's chosen people.

King Nebuchadnezzar only saw a dream. He was still blind. But God gave light to the king's slave, Daniel, and made him become a guide to lead the king into the future. Daniel was born for a purpose, and Daniel was captive in Babylon to fulfill God's plan for God's chosen people on earth. Daniel's life in Babylon testified that "In the Lord's hand the king's hearts is a stream of water that he channels toward all who please him" (Prov. 21:1 NIV). Thus, Daniel, a humiliated slave had become a great prophet of all secular kings in his time. Regardless of how difficult his life circumstances were, God was with him. That is why neither the lion's cave, the king's palace, nor his prayer room could change the fate of a servant of God. He had faithfully locked his faith in God's everlasting covenant.

God revealed the mystery of the rise and fall of all world kingdoms represented as different metallic pieces of the statue in Dan. 2. Consequently, the world power switched from one kingdom to another such as it happened in the ancient times—from Babylonian to Medo-Persian, from Medo-Persian to Greece, and from Greece to the Roman Empire. Essentially, world powers are one, since they are human in nature; hence, the world powers are united in one statue.[42] We are living in the post Roman Empire—also called *the end time*—that has a mixture between iron-clay feet until the stone from heaven that comes to strike down the whole image in God's appointed time and the Lord will reign forever in God's new established kingdom.

The Bible illustrates the essential history of humanity, and how human beings should deal with God and with each other in the mixed age of the end time. However, the influx of technology has changed our culture, our view of God and each other more than ever imagined in our human world. And this also changes the way we view the scriptures. We may one day experience a potential mixed Iron-Clay feet culture between humans and hi-tech machinery. Robots and humans may live together as AI technology is advancing in our present time and in the near future. The Mixed Iron-Clay Feet metaphor will be discussed theologically and semiotically in the next chapter. Human beings are stepping into the new adventure of a blended world—an amazing world that will mingle not only different human races but also humans and humanoid-AI robots (Human-AI) in the age of AI technology and cyborgs.

---

[42] Edward J. Young, The Prophecy of Daniel: A Commentary, 71.

CHAPTER 2:
THE MIXED IRON-CLAY FEET DISCUSSED
THEOLOGICALLY AND SEMIOTICALLY

In our world, natural and supernatural matters always exist parallel with each other. Though technology has made tremendous contributions to both science and religion, historians and theologians work to find connections between human history and biblical stories. A connection exists between science and religion to explain the creation of the universe, but not all topics can be easily connected because "problems arise as soon as one enquires about the relationship between 'science' and 'religion' in the past. Not only have the boundaries between them shifted with time but to abstract them from their historical context can lead to artificiality as well as anachronism."[43]

As humans become more civilized and human technology becomes more sophisticated, many Christians have a tendency to avoid discussing issues about science. Some Christians still read the Bible with a black and white telescope and do not dare to take new steps to discover the beauty of multiple colors from the amazing rainbow of Biblical metaphors. Likewise, some Christian communities are unaware that Daniel's *mixed iron-clay feet* metaphor has many potential applications, including a potential mixed Human-AI reality. As a result, Christians are unprepared to

---

[43] John Hedley Brooke, *Science and Religion: Some Historical Perspectives* (New York, NY: Cambridge University Press, 1991), 16, 22.

address the challenges between faith and culture in the age of overlapping humanity and AI technology.

However, God revealed to Nebuchadnezzar an image of a human in the metallic forms that changed from the most valuable metal at the head to the least valuable metal at the feet as an example of changing of times that not only involved issues of power and authority but also the substantial increase of advanced technology in the human world.

After the Fall of Humans, an agricultural, musical, industrial lifestyle was developed under Cain's descendants. The Bible stated that "Tubal-Cain, who made all kinds of bronze and iron tools" (Gen. 4:22 NRSV). Obviously, metal production is a sign of technology in the ancient world. King and Stager point out that in Israel in Biblical times, "the common metals used to fabricate jewelry, ornaments, and other accessories are copper/bronze, iron, gold, and silver. . . Iron is valued for its hardness and strength. . . Ta'anacch' iron artifacts, dating from the tenth century, includes both tools (sickles, plow tips, blades) and weapons (arrowheads, armor scales)."[44]

In the time of king Saul, the first king of the Israelites, the Philistines prohibited the Israelites to practice ironworking technology in their homeland and kept iron advanced skills to the Philistines alone, so that the Philistines could plunder and dominate the Israelites.

---

[44] Philip J. King and Lawrence E. Stager, *Life in Biblical Israel* (Louisville, KY: Westminster John Knox Press, 2001), 164, 168, 169.

Now there was no smith to be found throughout all the land of Israel; for the Philistines said, "The Hebrews must not make swords or spears for themselves"; so, all the Israelites went down to the Philistines to sharpen their plowshares, mattocks, axes, or sickles. The charge was two-thirds of a shekel for the plowshares and for the mattocks, and one-third of a shekel for sharpening the axes and for setting the goads. So, on the day of the battle neither sword nor spear was to be found in the possession of any of the people with Saul and Jonathan; but Saul and his son Jonathan had them (1 Sam. 13:19-22 NRSV).

Though ironworking technology is complicated, scientists discovered the benefits of iron, its contributions to technology, and its dominance over other metals, and the Iron Age became superior to previous technological ages.[45]

McNutt claims that "technology and technological innovations have long been recognized as major contributions to the development of social and cultural systems and have tended to be closely related to crucial

---

[45] James D. Muhly, "How Iron Technology Changed the Ancient World and Gave the Philitines a Military Edge," *BAR* 8, vol. 6 (Nov-Dec 1982), https://www.baslibrary.org/biblical-archaeology-review/8/6/5. The technology of working with iron thus became far more complex than anything connected with copper or bronze. . . Iron was no longer a curiosity but one of the most useful resources in the crust of the earth. . . Iron emerged as the dominant metal, largely replacing the casting technology used for copper and bronze.

turning points in human history."[46] Actually, technology is advancing rapidly in our present time, and this is one of the most critical turning points in the history of human technology. This is the age in which humans innovate machines that mimic human brains and human-like forms.

In the first chapter, human history through the first four kingdoms—Babylon, Medes and Persia, Greece, and Roman—are described. These kingdoms are represented respectively in Daniel's interpretation by the metaphors of gold head, silver arms and chest, bronze thigh and belly, iron legs, and mixed iron-clay feet. Details of human history prophesied by Daniel's interpretation of king Nebuchadnezzar's dream provided an emphasis on God's authority over humanity; consequently, all kings and their kingdoms rose and fell in God's timing. The mixed iron-clay feet metaphor was also briefly described in the previous chapter; however, this metaphor has left many questions for both historians and theologians in searching for its full meaning within the setting of world history.

Each setting of human history has different scale of civilization corresponding to the technological age advanced in that setting. In previous technological ages, humans created machines as advanced tools to help people perform their jobs with less effort. This reduced human labor burdens. Today, humans desire to create humanoid AI beings not only to help people to reduce their workload or to

---

[46] Paula M. McNutt, The Forging of Israel: Iron Technology, Symbolism and Tradition in Ancient Society, The Social World of Biblical Antiquity (Decatur, GA: Sheffield Academic Press, 1990), 13.

exceed the limits of a human's physical strength, but also to learn, to live, and to be in love with human beings. Machines (*iron*) and humans (clay) as two different "materials" with significantly different "attributes," mixed together in the human world (*feet*), would have sounded strange and reprehensible to the biblical mindset; but it sounds reasonable as we embrace current AI technology. The more we blend humans with AI technological features, the more we create *a potentially mixed culture between real human beings and humanoid-AI beings* (*Human-AI Culture*) within the world of humanity. For this reason, semiotically, my interpretation of the mixed iron-clay-feet metaphor shifts now from looking at the biblical metaphor simply in terms of diverse human cultures to looking at the metaphor as the potential blending of humanoid AI and human beings within a significantly changing culture. As scientists and AI developers continue leading us into the future, we must responsibly learn to navigate the jungle of AI technology and cyborgs with all of their corresponding issues and consequences.

Artificial Intelligence in Our Age

Scholars have offered different potential interpretations for the mixed iron-clay-feet metaphor. I am suggesting that this metaphor represents the mixed kingdoms that continue to flourish today after the fall of the Roman Empire. For the purposes and scope of this dissertation, I will argue that the mixed iron-clay-feet metaphor points today to the sophisticated technology of our present time—Artificial Intelligence technology. Therefore, in order to look at what the metaphor means for us, we must first ask, "What is Artificial Intelligence?"

According to the online Oxford Learner's Dictionary, "Artificial Intelligence is an area of study concerned with making computers copy intelligent human behavior."[47] The online Lexico Dictionary defines artificial intelligence as "the theory and development of computer systems able to perform tasks normally requiring human intelligence, such as visual perception, speech recognition, decision-making, and translation between languages."[48]

As AI is advancing in our time, some scientists believe that they can create an AI machine in human-like form—a humanoid-AI robot—that has consciousness and self-awareness like a human. It even would have a "brain"— a neural nets system—that mimics a human's brain. Furthermore, with the rapid speed of advanced AI technology, in the next couple of decades, humanoid AI will be mass produced, and potentially, there may be a new community of human-like robots existing on earth. It is important for us to be aware of this, so that we know how to properly respond to that kind of culture if or when it occurs.

In our present time, the relationship between humans and humanoid-AI robots has been increasing in some countries such as America, China, Japan, and Russia.

---

[47] *Oxford Learner's Dictionary*, accessed September 20, 2019, https://www.oxfordlearnersdictionaries.com/us/definition/ameican_eng lish/artificial_intelligence.

[48] *Lexico Dictionary*, accessed September 20, 2019, https://www.lexico.com/definition/artificial_intelligence.

Humanoid AI even garners citizenship in Saudi Arabia. The relationship between humans and AI is no longer mere hypothesis but a reality. AI technology not only focuses on advanced machines' benefits to human beings, but also promotes machines that resemble humans both in form and in response with a high level of intelligence and self-awareness. This type of sophisticated humanoid-AI machine has changed the degree of debate among people about the boundaries we are pushing as we compare actual humans with our new imperfect copies of human-like beings.

AI technology has rapidly developed, improved, and impacted every aspect of human life. God's gift of creativity in humanity has given us ways to hone a remarkably developed technology. For centuries, technology has been used by individuals and governments to improve life, serve humans, and even to exploit or oppress others. The whole world excitingly welcomes the existence of AI—the highest level of technology that mimics the human mind and acts like an assistant to human needs. AI technology continues to develop and may escalate to where humanoid-AI robots may be mass produced. This would generate a new type of community. Humanoid-AI robots would work alongside real humans, live as next-door neighbors, become friends, or become intimate partners of humans. Consequently, as humans interact and cohabitate with AI technology, a potentially mixed culture of real humans and humanoid-AI machines may come into existence.

Semiotically, I suggest that the mixed iron-clay feet metaphor from Nebuchadnezzar's dream represents for us today a new mixed culture in which not only human races are blended together but also humans and humanoid-AI robots. A so-called Human-AI culture is formed. A future age of Artificial Intelligence (AI) and cyborgs is coming, and the Church will need to explore the ethics and repercussions of this new kind of community.

No one can predict what might happen as human technology fully expands to its potential, especially when AI technology is rapidly developing. Nevertheless, the path of human civilization, which has led up to the most sophisticated technology in our time, will produce some amazing changes in the human world as AI technology advances in the next couple of decades. More theological details, as well as a semiotic view of this mixed iron-clay-feet metaphor, will be discussed later in this chapter.

THE MIXED IRON-CLAY FEET DISCUSSED THEOLOGICALLY

Daniel described the fourth kingdom:

> There shall be a fourth kingdom, strong as iron; just as iron crushes and smashes everything, it shall crush and shatter all these. As you saw the feet and toes partly of potter's clay and partly of iron, it shall be a divided kingdom; but some of the strength of iron shall be in it, as you saw the iron mixed with the clay. As the toes of the feet were part iron and part clay, so the kingdom shall be partly strong and partly brittle. As you saw the iron mixed with clay, so will they mix with one another in marriage, but they will not hold together, just as iron does not mix with clay (Dan. 2:40-43 NRSV).

As described in the first chapter, the fourth kingdom will last but will be divided into smaller kingdoms—ten kingdoms—and they will be partially stronger and weaker according to the attributes of the iron and the clay in the mixed iron-clay feet. The mixed iron-clay-feet metaphor provokes different thoughts from different scholars who have tried to make a connection between Daniel's interpretation and world history.

Some scholars interpreting the mixed iron-clay-feet metaphor point to Islam and the Muslim communities relating to Roman Catholic Church.[49] However, both Nelson and Newsom claim that the mixed iron-clay feet metaphor represents the intermarriage between the two royal families of the Seleucids and the Ptolemies.[50] This is based on Daniel's interpretation in a later prophesy:

> After some years they shall make an alliance, and the daughter of the king of the south shall come to the king of the north to ratify the agreement. But she shall not retain her power, and his offspring shall not

---

[49] "Revelation Timeline Decoded, The Iron-Clay-Feet of Daniel 2," accessed September 25, 2019, https://revelationtimelinedecoded.com/the-iron-clay-feet-of-daniel-2/. The iron, the Roman Catholic Church, helped Mohammed write the Koran and be revered as the prophet of Islam. The RCC has used Muslims to kill Christians and Jews, to protect Catholics, and to capture Jerusalem. But the Muslims kept Jerusalem for themselves and sought to conquer more land, so they don't mix well, and they have battled during the Crusades.

[50] William B. Nelson, *Daniel* (Grand Rapids, MI: BakerBooks), 91. See also Carol A. Newsom, *Daniel: A Commentary* (Louisville, KY: Westminster John Knox Press, 2014), 82-83.

endure. She shall be given up, she and her attendants and her child and the one who supported her.

In those times a branch from her roots shall rise up in his place. He shall come against the army and enter the fortress of the king of the north, and he shall take action against them and prevail.

He shall set his mind to come with the strength of his whole kingdom, and he shall bring terms of peace and perform them. In order to destroy the kingdom, he shall give him a woman in marriage; but it shall not succeed or be to his advantage (Dan. 11:6-7, 17 NRSV).

Green thoroughly recorded this intermarriage between the Seleucids and the Ptolemies. Ptolemy and Seleucus were generals under Alexander the Great. Ptolemy founded the Kingdom of Egypt, and Seleucus occupied the Babylonian Province. After being overturned by Antigonus, Seleucus fled to Egypt; Ptolemy took Seleucus in and helped Seleucus regain his power and recapture the province of Babylon. Seleucus then continued to expand his territory by conquering other nations such as Indus, Syria, and Assyria. He then grew stronger than Ptolemy. Egypt and Assyria were peaceful throughout the time of Ptolemy and Seleucus.

Then, Ptolemy renounced the Egyptian throne to his son, Ptolemy Philadelphus. There was a war between Egypt and Assyria, since Philadelphus' half-brother had married the daughter of Antiochus Soter who was king of Syria after overthrowing Seleucus Nicator. The war lasted until after Antiochus Soter's death when Antiochus Theos took over the throne of Assyria. To offer peace to Assyria, Ptolemy set up his beautiful daughter, Berenice, to marry Theos on the condition that Theos had to invalidate his marriage with his wife, Laodice, as well as give up legal rights to their two sons. Theos agreed to this marriage to make peace between Assyria and Egypt.

After Ptolemy died, Theos left Berenice and returned to his ex-wife, Laodice. Laodice did not trust Theos and killed him with poison, and Seleucus Callinicus took the throne. Laodice persuaded Seleucus Callinicus to assassinate Berenice and her son. Ptolemy Euergetes, Berenice' brother, was angry as he knew his sister had been mistreated, so he led his army to fight Assyria, killed Laodice to take revenge, and captured Seleucia, the northern king's fortress.[51]

Ptolemy Philopater succeeded his father, Ptolemy Euergetes, and became a great warrior. He was angry at Antiochus, the king of the north and Seleucus Callinicus' successor who invaded his land. Ptolemy Philopater's army marched against Antiochus' army and defeated Antiochus in 217 B.C.E. Ptolemy Philopater then died and left his Egypt to his infant son, Ptolemy Epiphanes. Antiochus thought it was a good time to invade Egypt again. However, before reaching Egypt, Antiochus had to cross the Holy Land,

---

[51] Oliver B. Greene, *Daniel: Verse by Verse Study* (Greenville, SC: The Gospel House, 1964), 418-420. Notice: "*Out of a branch of her roots shall one stand up…*" This means an offspring of the parents of Berenice, and refers to her brother, Ptolemy Euergetes, who succeeded his father, Ptolemy Philadelphus. He was naturally very angry about the treatment his sister had received, and he marched into Syria with a massive army. He arrived there too late to save Berenice and her son from assassination, but he took revenge by putting Laodice to death and capturing Seleucia, the fortress of the king of the north.

denoted as *the Glorious Land* (Dan. 11:16 NKJV)[52]. Antiochus conquered the Holy Land, the entirety of Palestine, and decided to invade Egypt with all his mighty power and his vast army. Ptolemy Epiphanes and the Egyptians asked Rome for help. Not being able to face the Egyptian-Roman alliance, Antiochus changed his scheme by sending Cleopatra, his beautiful daughter, to marry Ptolemy Epiphanes, king of Egypt, with the hope that Cleopatra would help him in taking control of Ptolemy Epiphanes and Egypt. However, Cleopatra supported her husband and saluted Rome's victories over her father. Being furious because of his daughter's behavior, Antiochus decided to destroy both Egypt and Rome, but he was defeated by Scipio Asiaticus at Magnesia in 190 B.C.E.[53] The intermarriage between Ptolemy and Seleucus had ended.

Because of this history, Nelson and Newsom's interpretation regarding intermarriage comes across as weak in regard to the mixed iron-clay-feet metaphor. First, this intermarriage did not represent the ten toes of the feet. In addition, the intermarriage between Ptolemy and Seleucus ended, and it did not last until the time when the rock was to be cut out from the mountain—the Redeemer from Heaven—to crush down worldly kingdoms and establish God's everlasting kingdom as Daniel interpreted (Dan. 2:44-

---

[52] New King James Version (NKJV): Scripture taken from the New King James Version®. Copyright © 1982 by Thomas Nelson. Used by permission. All rights reserved.

[53] Greene, 420-425.

45 NRSV). The intermarriage between these Greek generals ended following the rise of the Roman Empire.

Collins offers a different suggestion, "the mixture of iron and clay is taken to refer to the sharing power between Nabonidus and Belshazzar. The prophecy understood this way predicts the fall of Babylon but may have been of either Gentile or Jewish origin."[54] Collins' commentary about Daniel's interpretation of the mixed iron-clay feet could not be considered accurate, since Daniel prophesied that after the fall of Babylon, there would be yet another kingdom, less valuable but inferior to the Babylonian kingdom (Dan. 2:39 NRSV). Collins' view of the two Babylonian kings after Nebuchadnezzar's death is not suitable with Daniel's interpretation, as both Nabonidus and Belshazzar were rulers of the same kingdom, Babylon. Both Nabonidus and Belshazzar died, and the Babylonian kingdom never lasted until the time when the stone cut out of the mountain crushed the kingdoms, as it is interpreted by Daniel (Dan. 2:44-45 NRSV).

According to Green, the two legs represent the eastern and the western divisions of the Roman Empire. The eastern capital was Constantinople and the western capital was Rome.[55] Matthew added, "the Roman empire branched into ten kingdoms, as the toes of these feet. Some were weak as clay, others were strong as iron. Endeavors to unite the

---

[54] John J. Collins, Daniel: A Commentary on the Book of Daniel, 169.

[55] Greene, 94.

empires were in vain."[56]

Benson and others have similar views of the mixed iron-clay feet. They believe that the ten toes of the statue represent the divided kingdom of the ten nations which rose up from the Roman Empire. They embraced different interests and political desires. They mixed together but could not be united together.[57]

Some biblical scholars such as Hawker and Henry agree that the iron-clay-feet metaphor symbolized the post-Roman Empire—the on-going of the last earthly kingdom before the stone from Heaven would destroy all worldly kingdoms and establish God's everlasting kingdom in the end time.[58]

---

[56] "Matthew Henry's Concise Commentary: Daniel 2:31," *BibleHub.com*, accessed October 15, 2019, https://biblehub.com/commentaries/mhc/daniel/2.htm.

[57] "The Prophecy of Daniel 2," in *Signs of the End Time.* See also "Benson Commentary: Daniel 2:40-43," in *BibleHub.com,* accessed Ocober 15, 2019, https://biblehub.com/commentaries/benson/daniel/2.html.

[58] End Time Prophesy, "Kingdoms of Nebuchanezzar's Image," accessed October 25, 2019, http://www.end-times-prophecy.org/end-time-kingdom.html. What about the toes? Some believe these to be the ten kingdoms that emerged after the fall of the Roman Empire. . . The feet show us that from the division of Rome the world would remain partly broken until the second coming. See also StudyLight, "Bible Commentaries: Hawker's Poor Man's Commentary Daniel 2," accessed Octoder 25, 2019, https://www.studylight.org/commentaries/pmc/daniel-2.html#37. The fourth, which was denoted by the legs and the feet of iron, represented the Roman, and which remained unitil that stone cut without hands, meaning the Lord Jesus Christ, the humblest, and lowliest of the sons of men, came to establish his glorious kingdom, and fill the earth. See Bible

Metaphors often carry multiple meanings, which can be interpreted in various ways depending upon different perspectives of biblical and historical scholars, how scholars look at a historical incident, and express points of view that sound reasonable to biblical prophesies. As a result, scholars offer several interpretations representing the mixed iron-clay feet metaphor as described previously. One interpretation suggests that the mixed iron-clay feet metaphor represents the sharing power between Nabonidus and Belshazzar after Nebuchadnezzar's death. Another proposes that the mixed iron-clay feet metaphor represents the cooperated power of Muslims and Roman Catholic Church to persecute Christians and the Jews in Roman time. Some others consider this mixed iron-clay as the long intermarriage between Ptolemy and Seleucus families. Still others suggest that the mixed iron-clay feet metaphor symbolizes the post-Roman-Empire's divided kingdoms that keep on going until the rock cut out from Heaven crushes all earthly kingdoms and establishes God's everlasting Kingdom in the end time.

Though nothing could be a perfect interpretation unless it would be proven by human history, I choose the last suggestion, but I will focus on the mix culture between real human beings and humanoid-AI robots—(Human AI)—in the age of advanced AI technology and cyborgs.

Hub, "Matthew Henry's Concise Commentary," https://biblehub.com/commentaries/daniel/2-33.htm. The legs and feet of iron signified the Roman empire. The Roman empire branched into ten kingdoms, as the toes of these feet. Some were weak as clay, others strong as iron. Endeavours have often been used to unite them, for strengthening the empire, but in vain.

THE MIXED IRON-CLAY FEET DISCUSSED
SEMIOTICALLY

Is it possible that we are living in a similar empire of mixed iron-clay feet today? This empire will mix between the strong and the weak of unrelated materials—the iron and the clay. In the parable, the two materials were blended, but they were not firmly adhering together, were easily broken, and in fact were separated in their due time as Daniel interpreted the dream.

As clay and iron blended together in the feet of the statue but never stuck together, similarly, human beings are going to be working alongside and living together with AI machines, but they would never stick well together, even though AI machines will bear human-like forms and have an AI 'brain'—an AI neural network. When AI technology fully expands to its full potential, humanoid AI robots will be mass produced. I suggest that a new mixed culture of real human beings and humanoid-AI robots—Human-AI culture—will potentially come into existence. This scenario feels suitable to a semiotic view of the mixed iron-clay feet reality in Daniel's interpretation.

Since the time AI technology was first developed until our present time, it has played an important role in the human world, and it impacts every aspect of human life. Harris notes that "science fiction writers and moviemakers have created these fascinating visions of what a future with intelligent machines might be like. Often, they involve robots that look and act like people or computers that suddenly take on a life of their own. These images are exciting, but sometimes pretty scary."[59]

Unlike in the past, many current global leaders focus on AI technology, and this has been addressed by the Russian President Vladimir Putin: "The nation that leads in AI 'will be the ruler of the world.'. . . Artificial intelligence is the future, not only for Russia, but for all humankind."[60] While world leaders and hi-tech companies compete to create AI technology, this paper will explain why a picture of a potentially mixed Human-AI culture could possibly exist in the human world in the near future. The church must face the reality of AI technological development as humanoid AI becomes popular and extends beyond our imagination. Even though God is the same yesterday, today, and forever, the world of humanity keeps changing, and technology keeps upgrading. Christians must be prepared to face this new mixed Human-AI culture and to learn to faithfully communicate that God is in control no matter what happens in the age of AI technology and cyborgs.

Clay Metaphor

According to Wendy McMillan, "The definition of *dust* in Hebrew, according to Strong's dictionary, is

---

[59] Michael C. Harris, *Artificial Intelligence* (New York, NY: Marshall Cavendish Benchmark, 2014), 4.

[60] James Vincent, "Putin Says the Nations That Leads in AI 'Will Be the Ruler of the World'," accessed December 10, 2018, https://www.theverge.com/2017/9/4/16251226/russia-ai-putin-rule-the-world.

(powdered or gray) clay, earth, mud, ashes, dust, earth, ground mortal, powder, or rubbish."[61]

Kelly Clark claims: "Muslims widely believed that the Quran unambiguously teaches that humanity begins with Adam, who was created from (depending on the Surah) dust, clay, or water."[62] Because clay is easily molded, easily broken, and very weak compared to metallic materials, in this paper, the clay metaphor represents human beings. Furthermore, my view of the origins of human beings comes from the Biblical perspective—The Christian Bible. Thus, my interpretation of the clay metaphor as humanity seems reasonable to most Christians, and its application to humanity is very popular in the secular world as well. The Christian Bible demonstrates that God brought humans out of dust, blew breath into the first human's nostril, and humankind became a living soul. Genesis records God's creation and the existence of human beings on earth: "Then the LORD God formed a man from the dust of the ground and breathed into his nostrils the breath of life, and the man became a living being" (Gen. 2:7 NRSV). This explanation may be acceptable as a reasonable metaphor even to non-Christians and scientists.

Actually, science itself isn't a problem to religion, and many scientists still believe in God. One survey reports

---

[61] Wendy McMillan, *Amazed Clay* (Mustang, OK: Tate Publishing and Enterprises, 2010), 14.

[62] Kelly James Clark, *Religion and Sciences of Origins: History and Contemporary Discussions* (New York, NY: Palgrave Macmillan, 2014), 235.

that "In the U.S., 76 percent of scientists in the general population identify with a religious tradition."[63] According to the Pew Research Center for the People and the Press and the American Association for the Advancement of Science, "about one out of every three scientists in the United States professed believing in God, a recent survey found. That figure is strikingly lower than the proportion of the general American public that say they believe in God (83 percent)."[64] But even if the explanation is less than scientific, the Genesis story serves as a ground to explain what sets humans apart from the rest of creation.

Being created by God's own hands means becoming a living being, a human being, who carries flesh, blood, a biological brain, and a soul. From the Creator's view, human beings carry the *'image of God'* as God said, "Let us make mankind in our image, in our likeness" (Gen. 1:26 NIV). It significantly distinguishes human beings from animals or other creation in the whole cosmos.

The metaphor of clay representing humans is expressed throughout the Bible. Job claims, "Remember that you molded me like clay" (Job 10:9 NIV). "I too was formed from a piece of clay" (Job 33:6 NRSV). Isaiah prayed, "Yet, O Lord, you are our Father. We are the clay; you are the

---

[63] Rice University, "Nearly 70 Percent of Evangelicals Do Not View Religion and Science as Being in Conflict," March 13, 2015, https://phys.org/news/2015-03-percent-evangelicals-view-religion-science.html.

[64] Michele A.Vu, "Survey: 1 in 3 Scientists Believe in God," July 16, 2009, https://www.christianpost.com/news/survey-one-third-of-scientists-believe-in-god.html.

potter; we are all the work of your hand" (Isa. 64:8 NRSV). Yahweh proclaims, "Like clay in the potter's hand, so are you in my hand, O house of Israel" (Jer. 18:6 NRSV). David says, "For he knows how we were made, he remembers that we are dust" (Ps. 103:14 NRSV).

For the same reason, I suggest clay as the human part of the mixed iron-clay feet. Every Christian can agree that clay symbolizes how human beings were created in God's mighty hands. In addition, the picture of human beings represented by the clay metaphor is popular not only among Christians but is also well-known in secular culture. The iron part of the mixed iron-clay feet metaphor will be discussed in the following section.

Iron Metaphor

Iron is a type of metallic material and is used to make equipment, metallic tools, metallic toys, or industrial machines. Iron can also be used in robotic technology as well. Makehow.com reports:

> Industrial robots are mechanical devices which, to a certain degree, replicate human motions. They are used whenever there is a need to reduce the danger to a human, provide more strength or accuracy than a human, or when continuous operation is required. Most robots are stationary, but some move throughout the workplace delivering materials and supplies. . . Steel, cast iron, and aluminum are most

often used for the arms and bases of robots.[65]

Scientists and technological developers innovated humanoid AI—a sophisticated human-like computer machine—which is made of metallic materials, with a chip—a non-biological brain or an artificial brain—so-called "artificial neural networks,"[66] inserted inside its *rubbery flesh*, and without a soul. Iron not only represents one of the strongest metallic materials, but it is also a symbol of a cruel spirit, a strong regime, a political system, or even the super force of abstractions such as religion or intelligence. For those reasons, in my semiotic view, the iron metaphor represents the humanoid-AI community in the age of AI technology and cyborgs for both the strength of their physical bodies, their super intelligence, and the "heartless" mind of humanoid-AI robots.

Being created by human hands in a computer lab for business purposes, humanoid-AI robots are industrial products that aim to generate more income and benefit for companies. A typical example is "the first commercialized robot, the Ultimate. . . which appeared in 1961. It was a simple robotic arm—a programmable mechanical arm made of metal links and joints—with an end that could grip, spin, or weld manipulated objects according to instruction set by

---

[65] Makehow.com, "Industrial Robots," accessed July 29, 2019, http://www.madehow.com/Volume-2/Industrial-Robot.html#ixzz5vqwPrLPt.

[66] Jayesh Bapu Ahire, *Artificial Neural Networks: The Brian behind AI* (England: AI Researcher, 2018), 55.

human operators. It was sold to General Motors to use in the production of automobiles."[67]

However, humans never stop making their creative inventions and periodically improve the pace of technology with great achievements beyond their imagination. Thus, humans strive to make machines that not only serve or depend on human beings for instruction, but also learn how to think for themselves with a certain level of being independent from humans. Consequently, "over the past twenty years, philosophers, computer scientists, and engineers have begun reflecting seriously on the prospects for developing computer systems and robots capable of making moral decisions."[68] As a result, humanoid AI and cyborgs were innovated. According to Clarke, "Cyborgs didn't come along until 1960, when the word was coined by Manfred Clynes and Nathan S. Kline."[69]

Though science and technology can create an AI robot in a human-like form, whatever form a humanoid AI robot is made into, it is basically a machine, a very sophisticated, good-looking, high-tech, functional machine. However, when AI technology rapidly advances in the future, humanoid-AI robots will be mass produced.

---

[67] John Paul Muller and Luca Massaron, *Artificial Intelligence for Dummies* (Hoboken, NJ: John Willey and Son, 2018), 183.

[68] Patrick Lin, Keith Abney, and George A. Berkey, eds., *Robot Ethics: The Ethical and Social Implication of Robotics* (Cambridge, Mass: MIT Press, 2012), 55.

[69] Neil Clarke, ed., More Human than Human: Stories of Androids, Robots, and Manufactured Humanity (New York, NY: Night Shade Books, 2017), x.

As humanoid-AI robots increase their awareness and adopt human behaviors through their deep learning skills, they will begin a transition into a new type of community, one of their own kind, and a new human-like culture with their own way of life. No one can predict the future and what will happen to the human world when human intelligence is reaching for the sky. What if this happens in the next couple of decades? The world will potentially become a mixed Human-AI culture in the age of advanced AI technology.

Mixed Iron-Clay Feet

A Potentially Mixed Human-AI Culture

Kevin Warwick claims, "Ongoing research aims at releasing an AI system in a body—embodiment—so it can experience the world, whether it will be the real version of the world or a virtual or even simulated world."[70] If so, there would be another human-like being coming into existence in the near future. Thus, the human world will not only have a human community, but it will also have another human-like community—a cyborg or a humanoid-AI robotic community. That better explains my semiotic view of mixed iron-clay feet as a potentially mixed Human-AI culture in the age of AI technology, advancing in the next couple of decades. Year 2050 is "a year that will see the world transform in big and small ways; this includes disruptions

---

[70] Kevin Warwick, *Artificial: The Basic* (New York, NY: Routledge, 2012), 10.

throughout our culture, technology, science, health and business sectors."[71]

We may be excited that AI technology has brought much comfort into our world, such as in helping humans with repeated tasks in a production line, helping surgeons to practice their brain surgical tasks more accurately, making our transportation system more efficient, or in other beneficial ways. However, this new advanced AI technology gives rise to many questions concerning life in our world today. When a humanoid AI is given an artificial 'brain' in its robotic body, what will happen then? Will humans stay in control when humanoid-AI robots surpass human intelligence?[72]

Having a newborn baby in a family raises many new issues for a newlywed couple. Similarly, the existence of the new face of humanoid-AI robots or cyborgs on earth will raise ethical, emotional, spiritual, even political issues in the human world. Perhaps, in the future, there will be huge changes in human culture in which the world of humanity is no longer made up only of humans but potentially will be a mixture between real humans and human-like beings—

---

[71] Quantumrun.com, "What 2050 Will Look Like: Future Forecast," accessed September 20, 2019, https://www.quantumrun.com/future-timeline/2050#technology0.

[72] Kevin Warwick, *I, Cyborg* (Urbana, IL: University of Illinois, 2004), 3. See also Warwick, *Artificial: The Basic*, viii. Artificial brains are now being given their own body with which to perceive the world in their own way, to move around in it, and modify as they see fit. They are being given the ability to learn, adapt, and carry out their wishes regarding humans. This raises all sorts of issues for the future.

humanoid-AI robots or cyborgs. How can we think of a way to understand the mixture of humanity and humanoid AI? It may be very hard for people to find a way of making sense of these new, strange half-human, half-machine inhabitants. And it may be hard to make sense of ourselves when humanoid-AI robots exist parallel with real humans in our human world. Moreover, humans will be frustrated in dealing with "their" humanoid AI behaviors, perception, self-awareness, emotions, and spiritual thinking. People may worry whether it will be safe to live among humanoid-AI inhabitants, or whether humanoid-AI robots will bring benefits or troubles to humanity. Furthermore, the most sensitive question is: Are humanoid AI going to take over our jobs, since they are very fast and offer cheap labor? Many questions about the daily life of humanity would be addressed regarding the existence of humanoid AI in that mixed Human-AI culture by the time our humanoid-AI "neighbors" live next door to us.

Certainly, some issues regarding science and Christianity would need to be addressed. Some people may wonder whether a humanoid AI carries the image of God, has a soul, or receives God's salvation. In that mixed Human-AI culture, some youths may want to marry an AI robot and wonder whether a human-AI couple will be able to hold their wedding ceremony in the church. Is it possible for an AI to be involved in leadership roles, such as being a pastor, a manager, or a counselor, when needed? Many Christians are concerned with the possibility of an ex-Google engineer building an "AI God," and whether it could be described as the "666" Beast in Rev. 13: 14-18 (NRSV)?

In every cultural shift, challenges and opportunities always exist parallel to each other. Some people focus on the challenges, get stuck in their struggles, and do not get through their life challenges; as a result, they accept failures. In contrast, some other people often look at challenges as great opportunities to bring fresh renewal into their lives, overcome challenges and successfully move on with a better life. Similarly, in a potentially blended Human-AI culture, a significant opportunity exists for the Church to define what it means to be fully human and to provide a redemptive, ethical, and theological framework for the benefit of humanity. The next chapters will cover these points in more detail.

CONCLUSION

God's story of humanity exists in a world influenced by technology as the metaphor of the metallic humanoid statue describes in Nebuchadnezzar's dream. The time of the rising and falling of human kingdoms exists by the hands of God. God is the author of human history, and God has the right to authorize certain people to be key characters for each chapter in the book of humanity. King notes, "the aim of Daniel is to encourage the people of God, to give them a prophetic lamp in the darkness, and to show the missionary side of things as the God of heaven rules over the kingdom of men."[73]

---

[73] Geoffrey R. King, *Daniel: A Detailed Explanation of the Book* (Grand Rapids, MI: Wm. B. Eerdmans, 1966), 25.

The statue in Nebuchadnezzar's dream changes its metallic values from gold to silver, silver to bronze, and bronze to iron, and continues with a mixed iron-clay material which reveals the rise and fall of the world kingdoms as Daniel interpreted it. Human history proved that world power had switched from Babylonia to Medo-Persia, from Medo-Persia to Greek, from Greek to Roman, and from the Roman Empire to a mixed culture after the fall of Rome until our present time. However, God never changes!

The mixed iron-clay feet have many different interpretations and it could also semiotically be seen as a potentially mixed Human-AI culture in the AI technology age. The whole world is rapidly moving forward into that mixed Human-AI culture in which challenges and opportunities open for both pagans and Christians in the human world. Many issues will come along the way in which we perceive and react to that cultural shift—as a threat or as a test of life. Being positive and proactive always lifts us up above the time and above the trials. Our Christian faith must lead the way, be the light in a world full of darkness and chaos, future unknowns and frightening uncertainties.

CHAPTER 3:
CHRISTIAN THOUGHT ON HUMAN-AI CULTURE

Nowadays, human science is extremely progressive even in a culture that tends to resist this form of change. The more technology that is developed, the more civilized humankind becomes. Science and technology have sought to make the lives of humans easier and more efficient. As a result, technology is becoming more and more advanced and scientists are constantly developing new inventions to meet both the needs and modern aspirations of humanity at every new turning point in the world of human civilization.

As the pace of industrial production lines increases and social life becomes more complex, people aspire to have machines that work with them in labor and can partly share the burdens of their daily work. For that reason, robots are developed because "robots are often tasked to perform the 'three Ds,' that is, job that are dull, dirty, or dangerous. Robots can crawl around in dark sewers, inspecting pipes for leaks and cracks, as well as do the dirty work in our homes, such as vacuuming floors. Not afraid of danger, they also explore volcanos and clean up contaminated sites,"[1] etc.

Furthermore, humans often dream to have intelligent machines that can empathize with people's thoughts without sacrificing clearly in communication. With that dream in mind, humans can begin to make a special machine that has not only sophisticated technology but also carries a human-

---

[1] Patrick Lin, Keith Abney, and George A. Berkey, eds., *Robot Ethics: The Ethical and Social Implication of Robotics* (Cambridge, Mass: MIT Press, 2012), 4.

like form. The aim of technology is to serve and support humans, yet in some ways it also reflects or imitates the human mind. Consequently, machines do not only carry out the *three Ds* tasks like before but also include the 'fourth D" task–the Deep Learning task—the intelligent task that mimics the human's brain. Thus, powerful artificial intelligence (AI) robots came into existence that carried human images, infused data, and held other vital information inside their artificial 'brains' (AI neural nets) within a physique similar to humans.

A bright, new achievement of science and technology has proved that the wisdom of mankind is reaching the pinnacle of a more sophisticated technological age than all the previous eras. This achievement is the innovation of a human-like artificial intelligent machine (humanoid AI), with a human-like voice and a significant level of knowledge compared to human wisdom. People may be afraid that humanoid AI will surpass human's intelligence. Masayoshi Son, the Japanese Softbank CEO thinks, "robots will not just outsmart humans but will have an IQ of 10,000 in the next 30 years."[2] Ryan from the Inc.com reports in *This Morning* Newsletter that "North American experts thought A.I. would outperform humans on all tasks within 74 years, while experts in Asia thought this would take only 30 years."[3] Kurzweil, Google's Director of

---

[2] Chris Ciaccia, "Robots Will Be 100 Times Smarter than Humans in 30 Years, Tech Expert Says," October 27, 2017, https://www.foxnews.com/tech/robots-will-be-100-times-smarter-than-huamn-in-30-years-tech-exec-says.

[3] Kevin J. Ryan, "Elon Musk (and 350 Experts) Predict Exactly When Artificial Intelligence Will Overtake Human Intelligence,"

Engineering, answered in an interview at the 2017 SXSW Conference that "by 2029, computers will have human-level intelligence."[4]

In contrast, some others may not believe so, such as Terence Mills—the CEO of AI.io and Moonshot, an AI pioneer and digital technology specialist. He claims:

> Artificial general intelligence as a concept is often misleading because all around us we see robots beating humans at various games and we panic. The problem is that those machines were designed to do what they did.
>
> In terms of actual intelligence, robots are way behind. Facebook's head of AI, Yann Lecun, says that in terms of unfocused intelligence, robots are currently behind rats, even. Even so, please note that rats are quite smart.[5]

Another scholar, Signorelli, wrote an analytic article about the capabilities of computer systems, with which he confronted the tough question of our recent computing era: *'Can computers become conscious and overcome humans?'* posted on the Frontiers website. Signorelli raised his opinion as follows: "this analysis will show the paradoxical

---

published June 26, 2019, https://www.inc.com/kevin-j-ryan/elon-musk-and-350-expertsreveal ed-when-ai-will-overtake-humans.html.

[4] Fox News, "Ray Kurzweil Predicts Computers Will Be as Smart as Humans in 12 Years," March 16, 2017, https://www.foxnews.com/tech/ray-kurzweil-predicts-computers-will-be-as-smart-as-humans-in-12-years.

[5] Terence Mills, "How Far Are We from Truly Human-Like AI?" Forbes Technology Council, https://www.forbes.com/sites/forbestechcouncil/2018/08/28/how-far-are-we-from-truly-human-like-ai/#16304feb31ac.

conclusion that trying to achieve conscious machines to beat humans implies that computers will never completely exceed human capabilities."[6]

This type of artificial intelligence is the hot debate among the civilians of our time. This controversial debate of AI going on now is dependent on the knowledge of those who are working in the field of AI technology and on how close they have been to experimenting with humanoid-AI robots. In fact, one question often asked over the past few decades inquires whether humanoid AI is not just a myth, but is a reality; would a humanoid-AI robot be accepted as a fully human creature? People wonder whether a humanoid-AI robot invented by scientists has consciousness and carries a human-like soul.

This question is not a ridiculous idea. Yet this concept seems only to bring head-shakes or dismissive laughter to those who are not aware of the rapid development of the science and technology dynasty. Every day, artificial intelligence and science continue to strike for the clouds like the story of the ancient Babel Tower in the Bible. An example of these cloud-growing developments lies in the human ideology of a world that computes important information and events through technology such as iCloud.

In front of the rapidly growing threshold of human civilization, there must be many changes in human society when human-like artificial intelligence is mass produced. In the near future, there must be controversial discussions concerning the human world which represents a mixed

---

[6] Camilo Miguel Signorelli, "Hypothesis and Theory Article: Can Computers Become Conscious and Overcome Humans?" *Front. Robot. AI*, 26 October 2018, https://doi.org/10.3389/frobt.2018.00121.

culture between two types of humans—real people and artificial intelligent beings with human form and human voice. Semiotically, my view of the mixed iron-clay feet from Nebuchadnezzar's dream in Daniel's prophecy (Dan. 2:19-45 NRSV) may present the merging of Human-AI culture becoming a reality in our time. This view may provoke an intrinsic conflict among Christian communities as many Christians do not believe that humanoid-AI robots could grow strong enough to form a new community of their own alongside real human community in the human world.

Moreover, what is the significant difference between humankind and human-like intelligence that has created this wave of controversy? The aim of this chapter is to present God's creation in the Garden of Eden in contrast to scientists' innovation in the computer labs and to define what it means to be fully human concerning Christianity's perspective in the age of AI technology and cyborgs.

CREATION AND THE RISE OF HUMANOID AI BEINGS

In the book *The Rise and Fall of Adam and Eve*, Greenblatt said: "Humans cannot live without stories."[7] On the one hand, without stories, life in this world is tasteless and boring. On the other hand, if there are too many stories, this life is frisky and tricky. If the same story is compared under many different perspectives, it becomes more problematic and more complex. Particularly, stories that are discussed in terms of scientific (physical) and religious

---

[7] Stephen Greenblatt, *The Rise and Fall of Adam and Eve* (New York: W.W. Norton, 2017), 2.

(spiritual) examinations sometimes create even more problems. Brook claims that the future of human history depends on each generation's judgement of the proper connection between science and religion; and their implications in the human living environment will reopen the issues with different perspectives from each generation.[8]

In previous ages, technology has helped our ancestors to survive through hunting experiences, through their agricultural developments that led them from the wandering land into the gathering tribes in villages, towns, and from there to the formation of their own human communities on earth. Technological development has continued growing together with human history. Beside human convenience and comforts, wars and power are other reasons to push technology to reach for higher and higher levels of creative innovation. As a result, technology has served both humanity's benefits and humanity's selfishness.

As Daniel interpreted, the metallic statue in Nebuchadnezzar's dream changed from one metal to another metallic type. Similarly, human technology has been changing from one technology age to another one throughout human history—the stone age to the bronze age, and to the iron age.[9] From the ancient time to the post-modern time,

---

[8] John Hedley Brooke, *Science and Religion: Some Historical Perspectives* (New York, NY: Cambridge University Press, 2014), 1-2.

[9] Biography Online, "Major Periods in Human History," accessed September 30, 2019, https://www.biographyonline.net/different- periods-in-history/. **Stone Age (50,000–3000 BCE):** The Stone Age refers to the broad range of 'pre-history' which lasted from approx 30,000 BC to 6,000BC, where the first metals started to be used. In the stone age, the use of metals was scarce, and the most common building materials and weapons were

technology has become the main tool for kings and rulers not only to protect their kingdoms but also to conquer others. The more technology progresses, the better human world is civilized, and the worse humans' fear is increased. Technology has not only produced advanced machines to meet humans' needs, but has also brought forth metallic machetes, bayonets, and various types of machine guns and military weapons that empower kings or rulers to enslave other weaker people or even to destroy human lives.

Furthermore, technology has not stopped at the phase of basic "laboring" machines but has been transformed into so-called "neighboring" machines—machines that can think, talk, learn, and even bear human-like images. These humanoid machines can become human partners—that can share not only human physical heavy burdens, but also human emotional, mental, and psychological features. Consequently, artificial intelligent technology has arisen to carry out human dreams, to satisfy human needs and to fill up the brokenness and emptiness in human relationships. As God builds relationship with humans through creation, likewise, humans are building relationships with humanoid-AI beings through technological invention. The invention by

---

wood and stone. **Bronze Age (3000–1300 BCE)** The Bronze age refers to the broad period of history when cultures in Europe, Asia and other parts of the world made the first uses of bronze, from mining copper and tin. Bronze enabled more powerful tools and weapons. It was an age where the first writing systems became devised and used. **Iron Age (1200–230 BCE)** The iron age was a period of economic development, where iron and steel enabled a greater use of metal tools which were stronger than previous Bronze Age items. The era led to developments in agricultural production, and we see the first evidence of written manuscripts, which includes great religious texts such as the Indian Vedas, (Sanskrit), and the Hebrew Bible.

humans of new human-like machine beings mirrors God's creation of real human beings.

God's creation and scientists' innovations have no conflicts if humans clearly understand the distinction between the limits of scientists' skillful innovations compared to God's real creation. Rice University reports:

> Findings from the recently completed study 'Religious Understandings of Science (RUS)' reveal that despite many misconceptions regarding the intersection of science and religion, nearly 70 percent of evangelical Christians do not view the two as being in conflict with each other. . . . In the U.S., 76 percent of scientists in the general population identify with a religious tradition. Only 15 percent of Americans and 14 percent of evangelicals agree that modern science does more harm than good.
>
> Rice sociologist Elaine Howard Eklund said: "Although many politicians and the media at large portray evangelicals as distrustful of science, we found that this is more myth than reality."[10]

People should never reject the remarkable milestones of scientific achievements. Similarly, people should not deny the phenomenal creation of God's brilliance. Many stories have been told about scientific, creative innovations as well as religious stories of creation throughout human history. However, the two most applicable stories in human history today are the story of the Garden of Eden of

---

[10] Rice University, "Nearly 70 Percent of Evangelical Do Not View Religion, Science as Being in Conflict," Phys.org, March 13, 2015, https://phys.org/news/2015-03-percent-evangelicals-view-religion-science.html.

Christianity and the ongoing story of the computer labs of scientific researchers and technological inventors. Erns made a suitable proposal for readers who prefer scientific arguments to explain Christian beliefs, "the only way to bring Genesis into our world is first to understand the world of Genesis and what this book is trying to say in its world. Then, we will be in a position to understand how Genesis can be appropriated by Christians today as a theological statement, not as a statement of modern scientific interest."[11]

THE STORY OF THE GARDEN OF EDEN

Deborah and Loren Haarsma suggest that there are five different explanations related to the account of Adam and Eve. That is, Adam and Eve who are seen as *the recent ancestors, the recent representatives, a pair of ancient ancestors, a group of ancient representatives, or just a symbolic.*[12] I choose the first interpretation—*the recent*

---

[11] Peter Enns, The Evolution of Adam: What the Bible Does and Doesn't Say about Human Origins (Grand Rapids, MI: Brazos Press, 2012), 36.

[12] Debora B. Haarsma and Loren Haarsma, *Origins: Christian Perspectives on Creation, Evolution, and Intelligent Design* (Grand Rapids, MI: Faith Alive Christian Resources, 2011), 230-231.

Adam and Eve: Five Scenarios:

➢ Recent Ancestors: Adam and Eva were specially created about 10,000 years ago and were the first humans. All humans today have descended from them.
➢ Recent representatives: God created humans about 150,000 years ago, using progressive of evolutionary creation, and specially selected a pair of humans about 10,000 years ago to act as humanity's representatives. They chose to sin and their sinful status was applied to all humans.

ancestors—as the basis of God's creation in the Garden of Eden, since it bears the specificity of Christian theology about God's creation, and it is seen as the Biblical standard that most Christian denominations accept as the Word of God.

This dissertation will discuss the first interpretation—Adam and Eve who are seen as the recent ancestors, created about 10,000 years ago and were the first humans. All humans today have descended from them— since it is more applicable to my focus on humans and humanoid-AI beings.

The Creation of Human Beings

Let us imagine that, before the creation of humankind, God had a model of the finest and most noble creature to be placed on this planet, a creature meant not only to adorn the earth like so many other created species, but also to carry a higher purpose to interact with God. This noble creature would carry the image of God, whose heart vibrated

---

> ➤ Pair of ancient ancestors: God used natural mechanism to create pre-human hominids; then about 150,000 years ago God miraculously modified a pair of them into the first humans, Adam and Eva. All humans today have descended from this pair.
> ➤ Group of ancient representatives: God created human about 150,000 years ago, using evolutionary creation, and specially selected particular group and revealed himself to them. They chose to sin and their sinful status was applied to all humans.
> ➤ Symbolic: God created human about 150,000 years ago using evolutionary creation. No particular single even occurred in which all humans fell into sin at the same time, but many events happened in which various individuals and groups rebelled against God.

through the Creator's love, whose eyes presided over creation, and whose great mind sought to replicate the Creator. That is what God carefully and thoughtfully considered before shaping this fabulous being by the art of God's mighty hand, by the love of God's heart, and by the living breath of God's Spirit. The mark of God's fingers and the breath of God in this new lively and lovely creature transformed it into a spectacular species, a so-called human species.

In Genesis, five days of creation passed, and God still felt an emptiness when God did not see any creature carrying God's own image in order to achieve fellowship in this majestic, physical world that God created. Even the whole cosmos, which obeys the Words of God carries only the tangible beauty of a natural world—a touchable physical but sabotageable creation. It is a nature of herbs and plants, insects and animals, and a universe that carries a lifestyle of low-level survival laws. But it is a soulless world.

No flesh could raise its head toward the Creator with a mind made out of the material world. No part of creation was able to completely understand the interactions in the supernatural world of God. No flesh had a heart that deeply understood and could exchange loving conversation between Creator and creatures. Thus, God looked at the whole universe to find some creature in heaven, on earth, or even under the ground that could represent God, to rule over all creatures, and guard over the earth, but neither the angel armies nor the ruling forces of darkness could fit.

Suddenly, the Second Person of God–later to be called the Son of God, Jesus in the New Testament— appeared, illuminating the radiance over the whole universe.

The image of the Second Person of God gave the Creator a special model for the noblest creature that God tried to create—a creature that carried an elegant high-class image blended between the dust of the earth and the sacred spirit of the Heavenly Throne, between creation and Creator.

Imaginably, the amazing narrative of the Days of Creation could be retold in the form of an interesting dialogue within the Trinity God. As the Trinity was gathered, the Father said, "We need to create a kind of creation that is only a little less than us, presented with the same glory, and as elegant as our beloved Son. We will call them humans, and they will be our people because we have created them in our image."

The Second Person of God rejoiced and agreed to say, "it's lovely to have a creature that bears our image and can communicate with us, sharing the glory and greatness that we have in heaven, on earth, and under the earth."

Finally, the Triune God was excited about the decision to create a creature that would resemble God's image. God began to take dust to mold the shape of humans in God's hands, God did it so carefully that every fingerprint of the Creator was imprinted on every human finger. "Oh, human beings are already like us!" the Second Person of God said, happy to see people carrying God's image. He said: "from now on we will have creatures in our image, but how do they become like us in the supernatural relationship beyond the natural physical world of other creatures?"

The Third Person of God—the Holy Spirit—stepped in and embarked on the work of creating humans, saying: 'To have humans become not only a species of flesh, but a kind of species that is completely different from other creatures, a spirit of life, the breath of God needs to be infused in them.' Then, as the Spirit of life, the Third Person of God began to operate through all of God's aesthetic abilities to create a beautiful and vivid creature. The vitality of God through the Holy Spirit was infused into the human body. The Holy Spirit also conveyed into the human's mind a unique 'gray matter' together with the wisdom and knowledge that made mankind exceeding all things God created so far.

After God breathed God's living breath into the nostrils of the first human being, humankind became a living creature with a soul. Humans looked livelier and more elegant than other creatures. They had beautiful fresh smiles on their bright faces while their eyes sparkled like stars looking at the colorful radiant world that was drawn before them. They started talking to the Trinity of God with a knowledge that surpassed all creatures and with a language that brought them into a supernatural relationship in spirituality that no other creatures could. In particular, their hearts vibrated before the Creator's love every afternoon and every morning in the wonderful first Garden of Eden that God has created.

Genesis recorded how God created Adam, the First human being: "The Lord God formed a man from the dust of the ground, and breathed into his nostrils the breath of life; and the man became a living being" (Gen. 2:7 NRSV).

God also created the First female human, Eve.

The LORD God caused the man to fall into a deep sleep; and while he was sleeping, he took one of the man's ribs and then closed up the place with flesh. Then the LORD God made a woman from the rib he had taken out of the man, and he brought her to the man. The man said, "This is now bone of my bones and flesh of my flesh; she shall be called 'woman,' for she was taken out of man. (Gen. 2: 21-23 NIV).

This miraculous creation seems to have been revealed to King David when he was moved by the Spirit, the master in God's creative work, uttering: "What are human beings that you are mindful of them, mortals that you care for them? Yet you have made them a little lower than God and crowned them with glory and honor" (Ps. 8: 4-5 NRSV). Adam and Eve, the first human beings created in the image of God, carried in their *dust* body the breath of God, and a living soul. They were perfect humans in the eyes of God both physically and spiritually. The Bible clearly expresses this perfection of humanity.

If we focus on the end of each day of God's creative work in Genesis, after each day of creation, Genesis 1 wrote: "God saw that it was good" (NRSV). God evaluated God's creation work on the whole universe as "good." However, when God finished God's wonderful perfect art— "mankind," Genesis records that "it was very good" (Gen. 1:31 NRSV). Whatever God announces that 'it is very good,' it means that it is perfect in the eyes of God, and it means that God is very pleased with the perfect "human beings" that God created. It is the creation story in the Garden of Eden that Christianity has recounted throughout the ages, and it still will not fade away through all eternity as well.

THE STORY OF THE COMPUTER LABORATORY

After the Fall of mankind, humans tried to restore themselves to the noble image that they had lost in the Garden of Eden. Having inherited God's creative skills, mankind used their wise minds, their emotional hearts, their beautiful eyes, and their ingenious, creative hands to create precious literary works, vivid paintings, and sensual music. Humans even created virtuoso artistic sculptures to impart upon their descendants the images of their ancestors along with cultural and social changes according to each civilized bridge of humanity through each developed stage of human history.

Human capacity is constantly increasing according to God's creative ability bestowed upon them. Human society has glowed with new inventions in agriculture, industry, and technology. In addition, the achievements of advanced science and technology have helped humans to have a richer life, a more diverse life, and a civilization surpassing all other creatures. Human wisdom together with their profound technology has enabled them to play the universal governing role that God has imparted to them.

However, the more humans have connected to science and technology, and lost their focus on God, humans have become lonely—lonely to the point of struggling with human relationships. Due to this loneliness in their hearts, humans have become more connected to the technology they created, and they have formed relationships with objects, rather than with people. Consequently, humans have lost the "us in our image" part of creation and have developed communities with created objects rather than humans. To satisfy humans' desire of not being lonely, humans have begun to reproduce God's creative work and have attempted to create a human-like creature with the hope that their humanoid artificial creatures could be able to think, act like real people, and understand humans better. Thus, the story of the computer lab is born to give birth to machines that mimic humans. The new age of AI technology and cyborg came into existence.

The Rise of Artificial Intelligence

The idea of human thoughts that can be installed into machinery and artificial intelligence (AI) in humanoid-mechanical forms has existed from ancient times. However, Alan Turing, a mathematician at Cambridge, was recognized as the father of computers and the grandfather of AI through his tireless experiments with his computing tests. In 1939-1944, during World War II, Turing successfully decrypted the encrypted messages from the German's famous communication cipher machine—Enigma—with his British Bombe machine that he invented.[13] Turing often wondered, "which problems can be solved by calculation?" As a result, a Turing Machine was born in 1936 for use in theorical computer science. Turing also asked, "can machines think?"[14]

---

[13] Keith Frankish and William M. Ramsey, *The Cambridge Handbook of Artificial Intelligence* (Cambridge, UK: Cambridge University Press, 2014), 17.

[14] A.M.Turing, "Computing Machinery and Intelligence," *Mind* 49:433-460, accessed April 14, 2019, https://www.csee.umbc.edu/courses/471/papers/turing.pdf.

Since that time, many researchers began their focuses on creating machines with a level of intelligence comparable to human intelligence. In 1943, Warren McCulloch, and Walter Pitts invented a so-called "McCulloch-Pitts unit" which gave birth to "Neural Nets AI and computational neuroscience."[15] Until 1950, with all his enthusiastic efforts of exploring the possibility of a machine thinking, Turing published his first paper about the ability of a machine to express intelligent behavior equivalent to or indistinguishable from humans. Today it is known as the "Turing Test."[16]

Until August of 1956, at Dartmouth faculty's workshop, John McCarthy—a Stanford AI lab founder and an inventor of the LISP language—officially announced the name *Artificial Intelligence*. Herbert Simon and Allen Newell—founders of Carnegie Mellon University AI Research lab—also contributed "an AI planning

---

[15] Keith Frankish and William M. Ramsey, 16-17, 340. The Neural Nets branch of AI began with a very early paper by Warren McCulloch and Walter Pitts (1943). McCulloch, a professor at the University of Chicago, and Pitts, then an undergraduate student, developed a much simplified model of a functioning neuron, a McCulloch-Pitts unit. They showed that networks of such units could perform any Boolean operation (and, or, not) and, thus, any possible computation. Each of these units compared the weighted sum of its inputs to a threshold value to produce a binary output. Neural Nets AI, and also computational neuronscience, thus was born. . . Neural Network (artificial): A network of artificial neurons (simple processing units) that purports to mimic biological neurons. Artificial neuron networks may be used to gain an understanding of biological neural networks or for addressing AI and cognitive science problems (without being models of real biological systems).

[16] Keith Frankish and William M. Ramsey, 17.

algorithm."[17] The AI algorithm is compiled into a computer system to make a machine run and do only what it is programed to do. However, there would be a potential that a machine can learn, such as in the case of Arthur Samuel's checker playing program which later beaten its own inventor. Since then, the basic theory for "machine learning was born."[18]

Reynoso claims,

> From the 1950s forward, many scientists, logicians, programmers, and theorists aided in solidifying the modern understanding of artificial intelligence as a whole. With each new decade came innovations and findings that changed people's fundamental knowledge of the field of artificial intelligence and how historical advancements have catapulted AI from being an unattainable fantasy to a tangible reality for current and future generations.[19]

---

[17] Keith Frankish and William M. Ramsey, 18, 339. John McCarthy, on the Darthmouth faculty at the time of the Workshop, is credited with having coined the name Artigicial Intelligence. He was also the inventor of LISP, the predominat AI programing language for a half century. . . Lisp or LISP: A programing language devised by John McCarthy in 1959 and subesequentlty developed into many variants. The language's features make it well suited for AI programming, and it has been widely used in the field.

[18] Keith Frankish and William M. Ramsey, 19. Machine learning, later to become a major subfield of AI, began with Arthur Samuel's checker playing program (1959). Though Samuel was initially able to beat his program, after a few months of learning, it is said that he never won another game from it. Machine learning was born.

[19] Rebecca, Reynoso, "The Complete History of Artificial Intelligence," accessed April 12, 2019, http://learn.g2crowd.com/history-of-artificial-intelligence.

Many AI machines developed in the last several decades, which are simple robotic machines. William Grey Walker was a pioneer in making two wheeled robots, called "tortoises."[20] Then, "in 1954 George Devol invented the first digitally operated and programmable robot called the Unimate. In 1956, Devol and his partner Joseph Engel Berger formed the world's first robot company. In 1961, the first industrial robot, Unimate, went online in a General Motors automobile factory in New Jersey."[21]

Instead of building robots to use for dirty, heavy, dangerous, or tedious jobs that are not suitable for humans such as in a production line, assembly, and packaging of consumer and industrial goods, or to use in delivery or transportation, humans dream to create a humanoid machine with a brain and a way of thinking like a real person. Zarkadakis describes the human dream in his book *In Our Image* as follows:

> Perhaps we seek to construct Artificial Intelligence out of some instinctive impulse, rather than the utilitarian need for it. Consider the ramifications of a conscious machine: one that thinks and feels like human, an 'electronic brain' that dreams and ponders its own existence, falls in and out of love, writes sonnets under the light moon, laughs when happy, and cries when sad.[22]

---

[20] Keith Frankish and William M. Ramsey, 270.

[21] Marry Bellis, "Who Pioneered Robotics?" ThoughtCo., updated February 03, 2019, https://www.thoughtco.com/timeline-of-robots-1992363.

[22] George Zarkadakis, In Our Image: Savior or Destroyer? The History and Future of Artificial Intelligence (New York, NY: Pegasus Books, 2015), xviii.

As humans have often failed in their relationships with each other, they tried to find a solution to fill up their brokenness. Somehow, working with machines has given humans new thoughts as to whether it would be easier to build new relationships with machines or other hi-tech objects. To fulfil this dream of humankind, neuroscience has continued to develop and improved AI technology that will integrate humanoid-AI robots with AI 'brains'—Neural Nets AI—in human-like forms.

The most human-like AI robot today is Sophia, a recent product of Hanson Robotics Company. According to Wikipedia, "Sophia is a social humanoid robot developed by Hong Kong based company Hanson Robotics. Sophia was activated on February 14, 2016 and made its first public appearance at the South by Southwest Festival (SXSW) in mid-March 2016 in Austin, Texas, United States."[23] Hanson Robotics describes: "Sophia embodies Hepburn's classic beauty: porcelain skin, a slender nose, high cheekbones, an intriguing smile, and deeply expressive eyes that seem to change color with the light."[24]

However, "experts who have reviewed the robot's open-source code, which is posted on GitHub, agree that the most apt description of Sophia is probably a Chatbot with a

---

[23] Wikipedia, "Sophia (Robot)," accessed September 20, 2018, https://en.wikipedia.org/wiki/Sophia_(robot).

[24] Zara Stone, "Everything You Need to Know about Sophia, the World's First Robot Citizen," *Forbes*, November 7, 2017, https://www.forbes.com/sites/zarastone/2017/11/07/everything-you-need-to-know-about-sophia-the-worlds-first-robot-citizen/#2dc18e9146fa.

face."[25] Thus, it means the world's most human-like AI robot—which is the most advanced product of human hands and human intelligence, and achieved the legal citizenship in Saudi Arabia—still could not be a fully human being. In other words, Sophia, the ancestor of a humanoid-AI robot, is still just a modern machine with a face that replicates the image of a model. Sophia, this human-like female robot, is a soulless mechanical model, according to Japanese experts.

Controversial Discussion on Artificial Intelligence

Though Sophia is not a perfect humanoid-AI robot, her appearance in public has caused a wave of controversial debates about the kinds of opportunities and challenges that humanity will face in the age of AI technology and cyborgs. Throughout human history of civilization, technology has bestowed lots of benefits to our human world. Nevertheless, the world could not avoid crisis by human errors due to the misuses and the abuses of technology. Human technology is rapidly advanced, with machines, such as autonomous killing guns or biological weapons.

The most critical matter that provokes controversial ethical discussions between science and religion, specifically, Christianity, is "what does it means to be fully human in the age of AI technology?" Scientists and technology inventors have tried to create a humanoid AI with human-like appearance and with an AI "brain" to acquire sensory feelings and consciousness like real people.

---

[25] Dave Gershgorn, "Inside the Mechanical Brain of the World's First Robot Citizen," Quartz November 12, 2017, https://qz.com/1121547/how-smart-is-the-first-robot-citizen/.

Could there be a compromise between science and Christianity in defining a creature to be fully human? Erns notes "Science and Scripture speaks two different languages and accomplish quite different things."[26]

So, what will the future of our life within the age of AI technology look like, where humans are living together with a new kind of humanoid-AI creatures? Assuming that humanoid AI is progressively developed to the level of human intelligence or potentially surpassing human intelligence level, how will we distinguish between humans and humanoid-AI beings—God's creation and human invention? The only matter is not who will be more intelligent than whom, but the core of ethical discussion will be about what makes a creature fully human. In this chapter, I will also discuss my Christian perspective regarding the query of what it means to be fully human.

WHAT DOES IT MEAN TO BE FULLY HUMAN?

In response to the question of "what does it mean to be fully human?" this session explores the three Christian ethics—the image of God, the matter of the flesh, and the matter of the soul in humanity. These three things underpin my purpose to lead readers into an imaginative future in which the human world will potentially be blended with both humans and humanoid-AI robots—my semiotics view of the mixed iron-clay feet metaphor from Nebuchadnezzar's dream in Dan. 2:17-35 (NRSV).

---

[26] Peter Enns, The Evolution of Adam, 16.

The Image of God

First, to be fully human, humanity carries the Image of God. Carrying the image of God made humans more outstanding in all things, and nothing can be comparable, even from infinite to eternity. This image of God in humanness is so beautiful that the angels in the sky above, all things over the whole universe, and all the forces beneath the deep areas, are jealous and hungry for it. It is this image of God that distinguishes human beings from all other things.

Without carrying the image of God, humans are no more than other creatures and have no greater value exceeding beyond the angels and forces of the heavens. Without the image of God, humans have no authority to live out the right purpose of reigning over all the things God has created on earth. Without God's image, humans would have no clue of God's identity within them. It is because of the image of God in human beings that there has never been a case of mistaken identity between humans and other creatures created by God. This is the true nature of the creature that is fully human in the Creator's eyes, and this is also one of the fundamental beliefs of Christianity.

Haarsma and Haarsma suggested three broad views to identify the image of God in humanity— "our mental and social abilities... the personal relationship between God and humans... our commission to be God's representatives and stewards."[27] These features define human beings, the fully human condition that Christians honor and believe.

---

[27] Origin, 237-238. Theologians have given three general answers, identifying the image of God with: 1) *Our mental and social abilities.* Some look at the differences between animals and humans and

Another scholar, Noreen Hersfeld, describes the image of God from the three most prominent Christian perspectives—the substantive, functional, and relational—interpreted by three exemplary theologians, Niebuhr, Von Rad, and Barth. Niebuhr's view focuses on human "Nature and Destiny" through experience in actual living context; and he explains that God and humans share a similar characteristic quality that makes humans bear the image of God. Von Rad analyzes Genesis based on literature and history and explores the similar "function" between God and mankind. He argues that although mankind does not need to have God's nature, the image of God in humans makes them replicate God in sovereign acts. Barth begins with the nature of God through the Trinitarian theological lens and emphasizes the relationship of the Triune God. Barth describes that in carrying the image of God, we "mirror" the Trinity in our relationship with God and in our relationship

---

have identified the image of God in terms of our greater mental and social abilities. Humans are superior to animals in intelligence, rational thinking, language use, creativity, the ability to build social relationships and so on. Humans share these characteristics of God to a far greater extent than animals do. 2) *The personal relationship between God and humans*. Others have identified the image of God with God's choice to have a personal relationship with us. God has revealed himself to us, hold us morally accountable for our actions, and intends for us to live with eternally. It is because of this relationship that we carry the image of God. 3) *Our commission to be God's representatives and stewards*. Others have identified the image of God with our commission from God to be his representatives and stewards in this world. In ancient Near Eastern cultures, a king would put statues (images) in distant parts of his realm to indicate his sovereignty. God transformed this idea by declaring humans to be his *living* images on earth to represent his sovereignty and to act as his stewards. This understanding of *image* fits with the second commandments, in which God forbids the making of graven images of himself; humans are already his living images.

with other human beings.[28]

In our present time, the whole world is moving forward within the new technological age, the age of AI technology, in which scientists and technology innovators have tried to create humanoid AI in our human image. Instead of creating intelligent machines to help to make people's life more efficient and more comfortable, scientists and technology developers generate more complex controversial matters by introducing a new way of life through human relationships with humanoid-AI beings. We humans have begun losing our image to the machines, and potentially we may have exaggerated humanoid-AI beings beyond human intelligent levels.

---

[28] J. B. Stump and Alan G. Padgett, *The Blackwell Companion to Science and Christianity* (Malden, MA: Blackwell, 2012), 503. Each of the substantive, functional, and relational interpretations of the image of God arises out of a different methodology. For Niebuhr, the question of the image of God in human beings is considered in the context of a study of the human condition. He begins The Nature and Destiny of Man with an examination of human experience. Von Rad begins with the text of Genesis, and uses the exegetical methods of literary and historical criticism. Barth begins with the nature of God, considering the text through the lens of Trinitarian theology. These differing approaches result in three different analogies between God and humankind. The substantive interpretation posits an analogy of nature, that God and the human beings share some trait or quality that is essential to our being. The functionalist interpretation posits an analogy of function. We need have nothing in common with God's nature; we image God when we perform actions in God's stead. The relational interpretation finds an analogy of relationship, that there is a relationship within God that we mirror when we are in relationship with God or with one another. Each of these approaches locates the core of humanity in a radically different sphere. These three approaches also differ on whether the image of God is expressed individually or corporately. The substantive approach finds the locus of the image in the individual, while the functional and relational interpretations find the image corporately.

Jesus says: "the spirit indeed is willing, but the flesh is weak" (Matt. 26:41 NRSV). This comment of Jesus indicates that humans inherit both a divine nature and a human (vulnerable/weak) nature that make us dependent on God. Though weak and broken, humans still find our identity in God. We come from God and we belong to God. To be in the *Imago Dei* means we are dependent upon our divine creator. Humanoid-AI beings are dependent on humans and belong to human inventors.

Even if a humanoid-AI has an image of a human being, such as Sophia, a sophisticated AI robot that has a plastic face of a human model and may look as beautiful as a talking *Barbie* doll, Sophia does not have any real quality character comparable to real humans. Therefore, Sophia, the most human-like AI robot does not carry the image of God but has been described by AI experts as a 'chatbot' in a human face, or no more than an advanced computer in a humanoid image. Yet Sophia is the first female robot who has earned a citizenship from an earthly nation, Saudi Arabia, and has been accepted as a more valuable "human" being than many other female humans in that same country. That still does not mean that Sophia can qualify to be called fully human according to our Christian beliefs.

The Matter of Flesh

Second, to be fully human is to be created with real human flesh and blood. Carrying the image of God, humans carry in them a special form to represent God among all creatures, a physical body blended of both natural (flesh and blood) and supernatural (spiritual) elements. We inhabit this physical body of flesh and blood in a rib cage with bones and tendons. That's why God created humans so wonderfully to make the mark of every single finger of God in humanity. Genesis 2 described that God created mankind from dust, a flesh-and-blood species.

"The Lord God formed a man from the dust of the ground" (Gen. 2:7 NIV).

> The LORD God caused the man to fall into a deep sleep; and while he was sleeping, he took one of the man's ribs and then closed up the place with flesh. Then the LORD God made a woman from the rib he had taken out of the man, and he brought her to the man. The man said, "This is now bone of my bones and flesh of my flesh; she shall be called 'woman,' for she was taken out of man" (Gen. 2:21-23 NIV).

Pedersen and Lilley argue that "according to Christian anthropology, the full humanity and the true image of God is fully realized in Jesus Christ (Col.1:15; Heb. 2:6-9)."[29] In the New Testament, this is also affirmed again with the complete identity of Jesus as being fully human in His incarnation. In order to be fully human, Jesus must wear human flesh and bones. This is why Jesus came into the human world in the body of an infant as any other human on earth. "Look, the virgin shall conceive and bear a son and they shall name him Emmanuel," which means, "God is with us" (Matt. 1:23 NRSV).

---

[29] Daniel Pedersen and Christopher Lilley, eds., *Human Origin and the Image of God: Essay in Honor of J. Wentzel Van Huyssteen* (Grand Rapids: William B. Eerdmans, 2017), 21, ProQuest Ebook Central.

Jesus was born fully human and grew up physically, mentally, and socially among humanity. Luke wrote about Him: "Jesus grew in wisdom and status, and in favor with God and man" (Luke 2:52 NIV). John also spoke of the incarnation of Jesus as follows: "The Word became flesh and made his dwelling among us. We have seen his glory, the glory of the one and only Son, who came from the Father, full of grace and truth" (John 1:14 NIV).

In the *Let's Take a Walk* in Napkin Scribbles podcast, Dr. Leonard Sweet argues: "When Spirit become matter, God became flesh. There is nothing that elevate flesh matter more than Emanuel, God is with us, God becomes flesh."[30] The invisible God became visible through Jesus' *flesh and blood* body. That is what God wants to show the world—the true image of God in humanness. Haarsma and Haarsma support this: "Beyond all this, God chose to become incarnate as a human being, to take on our very form. Jesus Christ humbled himself and took on a human body. That act alone raises the significance of humanity."[31]

Flesh means our human physical bodies; our physical bodies signify us as mortal. It means human beings will have a beginning and an end of our fleshy bodies. Humans are born, grow up, experience happiness and sorrow, life and death, without exception. Using the language of bioethics, Eric Cohen describes the mortal nature of our flesh:

---

[30] Leonard Sweet, "Lets Take a Walk," Napkin Scribbles Facebook Page, January 24, 2019, https://anchor.fm/napkinscribbles/episodes/Lets-Take-a-Walk-e2sakm?fbclid=IwAR3diKS58_ZXlYG2_lIyvTcSfq2S_Up6kDTwH9U mBt02VBRH5L_uItv0DA.

[31] Deborah Haarsma and Loren Haarsma, 280.

Bioethics is about bodies. And bodies are capable of the most wonderful things—dancing, embracing, thinking, conceiving, laughing, giving birth. But bodies also declined and die. To be biological is to be mortal. We are mortal; and we are mortal because we are biological. Bioethics, at its best, reminds us of what it means to be biological—what it means to be born, to grow up, to make love, to have children, to grow old, and to die—always with the threat of having life suddenly taken away from us. In doing so, bioethics aspires to say what it means to live well as biological beings. It tries to connect what we must live with (suffering and death) to what we should live for (love and excellence).[32]

In contrast, scientists and technology inventors are trying to create machines in a human-like form. This new creature wears the most expensive sophisticated "flesh-like" plastic skin to wrap around its non-rusty iron frame or metallic skeleton. Humans call this new creature, a humanoid-AI being, as in the case of Sophia. The Biblical emphasis on "flesh" is more along the lines of σωμα, (soma) which can be meat, body, or flesh. This emphasis is on something living, something similar to the animal kingdom. Cohen describes the aim of AI technology in term of biotechnology: "The ultimate aspiration of biotechnology— or the biotechnology project—is to master and use the way our bodies work so that we might live as if we were not really bodies at all, or as if we could always make our bodies do

---

[32] Eric Cohen, *In the Shadow of Progress: Being Human in the Age of Technology* (New York, NY: Encounter Books, 2008), 49, ProQuest.

what we want them to do without fail."[33] That is why scientists and technology developers try to create a humanoid-AI beings which have a body to work tirelessly without rest, a non-declined physique without feeling painful, becoming sick or dying, and a 'brain' to remember every single good or bad memory without knowing to forgive and forget. Consequently, if *soma* is body, then the Sophia robot is not subject to what the normal human body experiences such as pain, joy, sickness, or touch. No technology innovators would create and keep the human *flesh and blood* in humanoid-AI beings. Therefore, humanoid-AI beings will not be able to experience fully human nature—fleshy life—as humans do.

The Matter of the Soul

Third, in order for the human body to function, the human body must have the vitality, the breath, the living soul. The Bible says that God blows breath into the human's nostrils and the human becomes a living being, that is, a living creature with a soul and life. So, to be a fully-human creature, that creature must have a living soul. The soul distinguishes people from all other living things, and a soul is the spiritual life that connects the Lord with the human beings in a way that no other creatures can. Having the Spirit of life gives humans a free will of choice that is the privilege that the Creator has reserved for humankind. That means, humans have a choice to choose to obey God to live by the fruit of the tree of life—the Fruits of the Spirit (Gal. 5:22-23 NRSV), or to live by the fruit of the tree of knowledge of

---

[33] Eric Cohen, In the Shadow of Progress, 49.

good and evil. That is why human beings were not programmed to automatically perform their actions against their free will of choice. We have an ability to choose between good and evil, to sin or to not sin, to obey or disobey God.

The soul cannot be created by a combination of materials or a series of mathematical algorithms. The soul cannot be created by the effects of the external environment, the products of a living environment, the changes of social culture, or the transformation of human civilization through the ages. It is the mystery of the Creator. It is not in the ability of any human to create it; it goes beyond this world of substance. Thus, from the beginning of creation to the present, humans cannot master their destiny. No matter how intelligent a person is, he or she cannot hold his or her breath once God reclaims it. The book of Ecclesiastes says: "Life, lovely while it lasts, is soon over. Life as we know it, precious and beautiful, ends. The body is put back into the same ground it came from. The spirit returns to God, who first breathed it" (Eccles. 12:6-7 MSG).[34]

If the soul is the breath of God and is described as a spirit, this means that the soul is not a material product but an invisible spirit, a spirit of the Divine God. And if a soul is the spirit of God, God alone can give and has the right to take it back. People cannot have the right to decide on the duration of the soul living inside their bodies. Humans only feel the presence of their souls when humans have the breath of God in their bodies. When the breath of God is no longer

---

[34] *The Message* (MSG): Copyright © 1993, 2002, 2018 by Eugene H. Peterson.

inside human flesh, or in other words, when the soul leaves the body, the body of the human will perish, because there is no spirit of life in it.

Today, scientists, philosophers, psychologists, biologists, and educators can come up with many definitions of the soul depending on the developmental trends of science and technology or according to the most wisely and timely concepts of sociological culture. Those definitions aim to distort the value of the souls that God has for humanity. In fact, even if people give their excellent products a real name—an artificial soul—it will work just like a trademark on a fake item to deceive the conscience of those credulous and unaware of God. The true value of the soul does not change in God's eyes.

If the soul were a product of science and technology, many famous people would still be living today, because humanity would buy their own souls if they could. A human life endures when the soul exists in the body; once the soul leaves the body, the human body returns to dust, rots away, and no one can possibly keep that soul forever. If scientists could create an AI soul, it would mean, they could create an eternal earthly identity.

Those are the three most important and practical elements to determine a creature to be fully human, accepted by Christianity. Those are indispensable conditions to distinguish between real and false human beings.

CONCLUSION

Nowadays, scientists and technology developers have discovered many new things to make the human world more civilized, to significantly surpass all other creatures, and to prove that *Homo Sapiens* is the most valuable species on earth, the carriers of God's image. The more humans increase in knowledge, the more humans dream to the limits of our imagination. Living with tremendous imagination, sometimes humans have lost perspective on reality. When humans try to create our image through scientific and technical innovations, we lose the image of God that God imparted to us in the Garden of Eden; or in other words, we lose our image through soulless machines that we created in computer labs. The more humans distort the noble image of God in us and let ourselves detach from God, the more humans contort and lower the image of us in machines. Consequently, we let ourselves attach to our own humanoid creatures, and lose our intimacy with God, and with other human beings as well.

Instead of defining ourselves in God's image, the mystery of being fully human, people try to identify who we are within non-human beings. As Zarkadakis suggests, "what better way to explore this mystery than creating things that looks like us, behave like us, speak likes us, and 'feel' like us: an artificial creature with intelligence made in our image."[35] The Christian view of a fully human creature according to God's vision is facing new challenges in the age of AI technology. In fact, the conflict between science and religion is becoming more intense, especially between evolutionary ideas of materialism and spiritual concepts of Christianity. Christianity never rejects the great scientific achievements, but also never agrees that science is *another*

---

[35] George Zarkadakis, *In Our Image*, 304-305.

God, since science remains human wisdom in discovering the mighty arts of God's creation throughout the universe.

As Christians, we sometimes need to face the irrational questions that scientists and technology developers have created in our time, such as if a humanoid-AI robot can carry the image of God or not. Does it have a conscious mind? Does it have a soul and is it saved? These and other sensitive questions regarding Christian thinking within a mixed Human-AI culture in the age of AI technology will be discussed in the next chapter.

In my opinion, Christian rethinking should recognize the important purpose of sharing Jesus' gospel by focusing on "how best to communicate and interpret in language that both conveys the hearts of that message and speaks intelligibly to their contemporaries,"[36] not on the divisive science and religion debate in the digital era. This positive direction will give ways for both Christianity and the greatest scientific new inventions in the age of AI technology to bring their best benefits to serve humanity.

---

[36] Paul Jersild, *Christian Faith in Our Time: Rethinking the Church's Theology* (Eugene, OR: Wipf and Stock, 2016), 2, ProQuest Ebook Central.

CHAPTER 4:
CHRISTIAN RETHINKING HUMAN-AI CULTURE

As human civilization progresses, our outstanding scientific achievements are something that should be respected and preserved for the benefits of humanity. Scientists, technology experts, and social leaders recognize those as remarkable milestones in human history. There is no controversy over these great scientific achievements because of the wisdom that God bestowed on humans beyond all other creatures in the cosmos.

Haarsma and Haarsma argue that, "God is the author of both revelations, and that nature and Scriptures do not conflict with each other."[1] In theory, Haarsma's comment sounds true and is a view that any one of us can agree on, because it speaks of God's sovereignty in all areas. However, they did not forget to give reasons for the controversy between science and religion: "Science is our human attempt to understand the natural world. Biblical interpretation is our human attempt to understand the Bible. Conflicts can arise because our human understanding of one or both books may be in error."[2] Throughout human history, the civilization of humans is a key point that makes humanity significantly surpass all things in this world. No creature created on this planet can match the great glory that God has

---

[1] Debora B. Haarsma and Loren Haarsma, *Origins*, 73.

[2] Debora B. Haarsma and Loren Haarsma, *Origins,* 74.

bestowed upon humankind. As humans, we all, both Christians and non-Christian believers are delighted to welcome the brilliant achievements of science and technology. These achievements have helped to improve the human world step by step, moving up the new ladder of civilization. The new civilization makes the new generation surpass the previous generations. Therefore, human life becomes richer, more prosperous, and more comfortable with each civilized bridge of humanity.

We always express the pride of being born as a human being, a true human being bearing the name the *Homo sapiens* [3]— *the* wise man—which carries a perfect physical human flesh far better than other creatures, and especially a conscience and a living soul. The rich gift of creativity that God has given mankind has made our little human brain contain a relentless imagination.

Particularly, in the era of artificial intelligence and cyborgs, scientists and AI developers want to step up to a new level that has never been seen in human history—that is to create a humanoid-AI robot, a machine with consciousness, that has a so-called *'soul'* within a body in a human-like image. This has been highly controversial in the past two decades.

If AI technology continues to develop rapidly to the point where humanoid-AI robots potentially spread into a

---

[3] Yuval Noah Harari, *Homo Deus: A Brief History of Humankind* (New York, NY: HarperCollins, 2017), 3. *Homo sapiens* – the species *sapiens* (wise) of the genus *Homo* (man).

cyber community, then social and political mechanisms will need to revise the rules for this new society. The whole world will have a different perspective when interacting with a new humanoid community that exists bilaterally in the human world. What does Christianity think of the new AI generation? Are Christians ready to answer what it means to be fully human? And is it true that consciousness and the soul exist in other creatures created by human hands?

THE FULL HUMANESS OF HUMANITY

In the previous chapter, the image of God, the matter of the flesh, and the matter of the soul have been the three main topics of my focus on my traditional Christian perspectives. Different perspectives of a new humanoid-AI community would not align with Christianity's view of full humanness in responding to this new mixed Human-AI culture in the advanced AI technological age.

In the future, educational, political, and social systems will apply many changes in the interests of humanoid-AI beings when AI technology moves on to the most sophisticated level of civilization. However, according to my traditional Protestant perspective on the full humanness of humanity, this paper suggests some rethinking of the Christian ethical framework in the mixed Human-AI culture.

The Image of God

One of the core beliefs of Christianity regarding full humanness is the image of God in humanity. The image of God in humans makes humans different from all other living things, because humankind has a conscience, a consciousness of God. That is why animals only act accordingly to their instincts in which they behave and relate to other creatures without facing any judgement of their killing action before their Creator as humans do. In contrast, humans act according to their conscience or their conscious minds—the spirit of God in humanity. The spirit of God infuses the knowledge of the image of God in humanity which guides humans in their behaviors with other human beings. So, the image of God in humanity makes humans aware that they are responsible to God when they are dealing with the image of God in others. Emmanuel K. Twesigye describes this as the "personal moral self-judgment and the rise of an inner moral conflict, guilt and experience of a spiritual dilemma."[4]

This human conscience in humans generates a guilty feeling inside them when they do something that conflicts with the ideal codes of conduct that God infused in their conscious minds. It is a kind of spiritual sensation. Other creatures do not inherit this spiritual sensation, and they never feel guilty when they kill each other for meat when

---

[4] Emanuel K. Tweigye, *Religion and Ethics for A New Age: Evolutionist Approach* (Lanham, MD: University Press of America, 2001), 138.

they are hungry. For humans, there is a guilty feeling inside our hearts when we mistreat others or take other people's possessions without asking for permission. Similarly, though a humanoid-AI robot is programmed with intelligent algorithms, there is no clear right or wrong guidance in their neural AI nets; they have no spiritual sensation in them, and they do not experience any guilty feeling or moral compass at all.

Second, the image of God in humans gives them significant access in their intimate relationship with God those other creatures could not achieve. When losing this relationship with our Creator, humans feel an emptiness in our hearts that humankind cannot express. We look to the tangible world to fill an emptiness, an inexplicable anxiousness, but it cannot be filled without God. Precisely that void is the presence of the image of God in humankind, a supernatural relationship outside this natural world that God has especially carved in the heart of humanity. An imprint of God's infinite love exists as a mysterious frequency in every beating of the human heart.

Third, the image of God promotes an idea that all humans are created equal in the eyes of the Lord. Thomas Jefferson once declared that "people are of equal moral worth, and as such deserve equal treatment under the law."[5] However, as he wrote this, he still owned 200 slaves as his

---

[5] Matt Brundage, "The Meaning of Thomas Jeffeson's Phrase 'All Men Are Created Equal," accessed October 25, 2019, https://www.mattbrundage.com/publications/jefferson-equality/.

personal property. If the laws keep changing according to cultural and social changes, then will human equality also be changed accordingly? Because of the image of God in humanity, during the Civil War, President Abraham Lincoln fought for human rights, "His legacy as Great Emancipator, liberated over four million slaves, scholars have generated a controversial debate on Lincoln's position towards race and racism."[6] His Emancipation proclamation has made America a great nation of liberty.

The image of God in humans gives individuals a precious value that cannot be bought or sold. If an individual or group of individuals becomes involved in trading human beings, that will be considered committing human trafficking, and they will be judged as criminals. People who get into this lustful business will face justice sooner or later in their due time.

In contrast, humanoid AI are created in human-like forms to be traded on the market. SmashingRobotics.com reports that in 2016, there were 13 advanced humanoid robots on the market for sale in the ranges from a few hundred dollars (DARwIn Mini for US $499) to a couple million dollars (Asimo for US $2,500,000). According to the report, "robots are no longer used just in industrial environments, factories, warehouses, and laboratories. They have become part of the society we live in, part of our

---

[6] Jorg Nagler, "American Study Journal: Abraham Lincoln's Attitudes on Slavery and Race," accessed October 25, 2019, http://www.asjournal.org/53-2009/abraham-lincolns-attitudes-on-slavery-and-race/.

lives."[7] However, a controversy has arisen as to why an AI machine needs to be in a human-like form. Some robotics experts suggest avoiding creating humanoid robots, since it will create more complicated issues for humans, and they consider human-like AI robots only suitable for sex robots.[8]

To answer the question "why human-like robots?", the Hanson Robotics company, the creator of the Sophia robot and a warehouse of both female and male humanoid-AI robots for sale, ran an advertisement on their home webpage that said, "Robots will soon be everywhere. How can we nurture them to be our friends and useful collaborators? Robots with good aesthetic design, rich personalities, and social cognitive intelligence can potentially connect deeply and meaningfully with humans."[9]

If a friend can be bought or sold, it is only a non-human "friend" that can be marketed online or at the shopping malls, such as our friendly dog, friendly cat, or a

---

[7] Smashingrobotic, "Thirteen Advanced Humanoid Robots for Sale Today," updated April 16, 2016, https://www.smashingrobotics.com/thirteen-advanced-humanoid-robots-for-sale-today/.

[8] Keza MacDonald, "Being Human: How Realistic Do We Want Robots to Be?," June 27, 2018, https://www.theguardian.com/technology/2018/jun/27/being-human-realistic-robots-google-assistant-androids. Some Robotics experts, including the University of Edinburgh's Robert Fisher, see the concept of human-like robots as ill-advised. . . Fisher says. . . Sex robots are perhaps the only case where there is a reason for them to look human.

[9] Hanson Robotic, "Why Human-Like Robots?," accessed October 25, 2019, https://www.hansonrobotics.com.

talky-baby-doll friend. The first primate astronaut was Albert, a rhesus macaque, which followed by Albert II, Albert III, Albert VI was launched into space.[10] They were all treated as a special kind among other animals that were tested for spaceship experiments. They were also really the astronauts' friends. They worked together as partners during important missions in the spaceship with human astronauts and were buried in honor when they died; nevertheless, they were never granted any citizenship equal to human beings.

If humanoid-AI robots are to be mass produced and will be everywhere as Hanson Robotics company predicts, there will potentially be a new community of Humanoid-AI beings in our human world. Would humanoid-AI robots obtain legal rights equal to real human beings in the future? Are *"These"* Us? would be a controversial debate for our new generations to come. This may not be the fifth generation, but the sixth generation and onward. One

---

[10] Wikipedia, "Monkeys and Apes in Space," accessed November 2, 2019, https://en.wikipedia.org/wiki/Monkeys_and_apes_in_space. The first primate astronaut was Albert, a rhesus macaque, who on June 11, 1948, rode to over 63 km (39 mi) on a V-2 rocket. Albert died of suffocation during the flight. On June 14, 1949, Albert was followed by Albert II who survived the V-2 flight but died due to a parachute failure, pulverizing him on impact. Albert II became the first monkey and the first primate in space as his flight reached 134 km (83 mi) – past the Kármán line of 100 km taken to designate the beginning of space. Albert III died at 35,000 feet (10.7 km) in an explosion. . . on a V2 rocket on September 16, 1949. Albert IV, on the last monkey V-2 flight, died on impact on December 8 that year after another parachute failure. His flight reached 130.6 km. Alberts, I, II, and IV were rhesus macaque while Albert III was a crab-eating macaque.

government has promoted a humanoid-AI robot as a citizen of their country. Sophia earned a legal citizenship in Saudi Arabia. Throughout human history, people promote anything to be their own idols; thus, giving an equal right of human beings to a luxury humanoid being could happen in any country at any time. The world is changing, and the value of human beings will also change according to national laws. As a result, *human rights* could be redefined *under the law*.

Finally, God created human beings to rule over other creatures, not to be oppressed by them or even subjugated by humanoid-AI beings. However, human history has proved that humankind has lost the right to rule all species as God's ruling representatives. As a result, people have revered casting idols made of stone, clay, or metal as their own gods since the ancient times.

When the Israelites were in the wilderness after Yahweh opened a miracle pathway through the womb of the ocean and Moses led them across the Red sea, they asked Aaron to make them an idol to lead them out of the desert while Moses was meeting with God on the Mount of Sinai. Aaron cast them a golden calf image, and the Israelites considered it a god that rescued them from Pharaoh and the Egyptians, instead of exalting Yahweh who delivered them from the yoke of slavery. Eventually, 3,000 Israelites died of their idol worshiping of that golden calf image (Exod. 32 NRSV).

Daniel once interpreted the fate of King Nebuchadnezzar after the king decided to transfer the glory that God granted him into a metallic human-like image. Nebuchadnezzar created a golden humanoid statue and ordered everyone in his kingdom to bow down and to honor the golden image he built (Dan. 3:1-6 NRSV).

King Nebuchadnezzar did not honor the precious image of God in him, instead losing his glorious image into a golden metallic image—the semiotic symbol of the best civilized technology of the Babylonian kingdom. God revealed to the king that he would taste the bitterness of defiling the image of God and would live as other non-human creatures, a taste of a non-image-of-God nature compared to the glory of the image-of-God nature. The metaphor of a big tree being chopped down in his dream represented the king's transition from a human life into a beast's life. The king's dream and Daniel's detailed interpretation are recorded in Dan. 4:19-27 (NRSV):

Belteshazzar answered, "My lord, may the dream be for those who hate you, and its interpretation for your enemies! The tree that you saw, which grew great and strong, so that its top reached to heaven and was visible to the end of the whole earth, whose foliage was beautiful and its fruit abundant, and which provided food for all, under which animals of the field lived, and in whose branches the birds of the air had nests—it is you, O king! You have grown great and strong. Your greatness has increased and reaches to heaven, and your sovereignty to the ends of the earth.

And whereas the king saw a holy watcher coming down from heaven and saying, 'Cut down the tree and destroy it, but leave its stump and roots in the ground, with a band of iron and bronze, in the grass of the field; and let him be bathed with the dew of heaven, and let his lot be with the animals of the field, until seven times pass over him'— this is the interpretation, O king, and it is a decree of the Most High that has come upon my lord the king: You shall be driven away from human society, and your dwelling shall be with the wild animals. You shall be made to eat grass like oxen, you shall be bathed with the dew of heaven, and seven times shall pass over you, until you have learned that the Most High has sovereignty over the kingdom of mortals and gives it to whom he will.

As it was commanded to leave the stump and roots of the tree, your kingdom shall be re-established for you from the time that you learn that Heaven is sovereign. Therefore, O king, may my counsel be acceptable to you: atone for your sins with righteousness, and your iniquities with mercy to the oppressed, so that your prosperity may be prolonged.

If Nebuchadnezzar experienced a transition into non-human life during his golden, civilized Babylonian time, how would it be if we also chose to transition from our fully human life into non-human life, the kind of humanoid-AI life that AI technology offers us? There would be nothing wrong with creating humanoid-AI robots to improve our economy, to bring comforts, and to benefit humanity. We now create humanoid-AI beings to replicate our image so that we get deeper into the relationship with them and participate in a meaningful intimacy with humanoid-AI beings instead of building our relationship with God and other human beings. By doing that, humans may taste the bitterness of Nebuchadnezzar's beastial life in the glorious field of today's 'Babylonian age' of AI technology.

Teich argues that the fate of humankind would depend on human decisions to reserve our control and power over machines or give up our power to them and allow them to take control over us. Teich also concludes that if we let the machines make all their own choices without overseeing them, at some point in the future, humanity could not be capable of handling the machines' behaviors. Once humans willingly promote machines to be rulers over humankind, submit ourselves to intelligent machines, and ask machines to help us make decisions, because we believe that machines are more intelligent than humans, we open ourselves up to domination. At that time, people may beg for mercy from those intelligent machines, because we have given machines the right to control the destiny of humanity.[11]

The Matter of The Flesh

Humans have dreamed to have something created in our image to test the limits of our human knowledge and wisdom, reaching for the sky like the story of the Tower of Babel in biblical times. In addition, humans thought that if we created a humanoid-AI being in our image and inserted all human knowledge and wisdom into its Neural AI Nets by

---

[11] Albert H. Teich, *Technology and the Future* (Boston, MA: Wadsworth Cengage Learning, 2009), 103.

our human hands, that humanoid-AI being may understand us better since it is our lovely and lively product, and it mimics us from the outside in. Zarkadakis describes the human dream:

> We strive to create artificial intelligence because we have been telling stories to each other about artificial intelligent beings ever since the Ice Age. For the ancient Greeks, these were about the gods who breathed life into inanimate matter. For the Romantics, it was electricity harvested from ferocious lightning during a stormy night. For software engineers of the twenty-first century, the ghost in the machine is code. With time, the lion-man has been transformed into a cyborg.[12]

Actually, whatever good or bad thing our human minds imagine that often happens sooner or later in human history since the human gift of creativity sometimes goes beyond human imagination. The beauty of the human imagination is always accompanied by unpredicted human errors through human carelessness and human pride. Most scientific and technological innovations we bring into the human world are basically aimed to serve the benefits of humanity. Even humanoid-AI robots, one of the greatest technological and scientific achievements in our time are still bound to this great purpose. However sophisticated and

---

[12] George Zardakaris, In Our Own Image: Savior or Destroyer? The History and Future of Artificial Intelligence (New York, NY: Peagasus Books, 2016), 306.

intelligent humanoid-AI machines or cyborgs will become, they are not real human beings since they do not carry the full humanness in their physiques that humans do. *A core belief of Christianity regarding full humanness is the matter of flesh in humanity.* First, this full humanness in human flesh tells stories of the beginning and the end of a human life, the birth and the death of a human being, the celebration of a new living being, and the good memory of a loved one who has passed. Every human being must experience this life cycle. This life cycle reminds humankind that our human bodies are mortal. Being mortal, our physical bodies are "subject to sickness, aging, and ultimately, death."[13] As the Bible declares that "the dust returns to the earth as it was, and the breath returns to God who gave it" (Eccles. 12:7 NRSV). Therefore, the full humanness of humanity is the combination of the visible human flesh (dust) and the invisible spirit of God (breath). These two cannot be separated in real human beings in their life cycle on earth. Physical death is the state when human flesh is temporarily separated from the soul before a human body is reunited with an immortal soul, the new resurrected human form in the future Kingdom of Heaven.

This human life cycle is the Almighty Creator's destiny for man after the *Homo Sapiens* species listened to Satan's temptation and fell bitterly in the Garden of Eden.

---

[13] Noreen Herzfeld, Nancy Murphy, and Christopher C. Knight, eds., *Human Identity at the Intersection of Science, Technology and Religion* (Burlington, VT: Ashgate, 2010), 127.

This fate might seem like a dead end in the eyes of mankind and the devil, but this actually is the mysterious plan that the Creator has pointed out to humanity behind the death of their imperfect dust body. That would be the resurrected body beyond death, a transformed embodiment associated with an immortal soul in the Kingdom of Heaven similar to Jesus' resurrected body after His crucified death on the cross which broke through the Hellish gate and raised Jesus up from His grave. The new human resurrected body would be a new human form, carrying both the visible and invisible states, attached to an immortal soul—either a living soul in the lively intimate relationship with God or a dying soul in an eternal separation from God.

Second, the matter of flesh regarding the full humanness is related to human sensation, the human senses. Humankind carries five senses in human flesh. Even those who have lost one or more of these five senses can still be considered fully human, because they are steeped in human flesh, in God's image. "It is a mistake to believe that having a disability makes life less worth living."[14] These five senses are hearing, seeing, smelling, tasting, and touching.[15] These five senses in human flesh make human beings and the animal kingdom adjust to their living environment, relate to their real physical world and other creatures, and survive

---

[14] Peter Singer, *Ethics in the Real World: 82 Brief Essays on Things That Matter* (Princeton, NJ: Princeton University Press, 2016), 206.

[15] Leonard Sweet, *Nudge*, 134.

throughout their lifespan. Herzfeld describes these human sensations as the "embodied intelligence" that the Almighty Creator applied to our human flesh, so that humans can "interact with both the material world and the human community."[16]

The *'dust'* part of human beings is molded by the hand of God and transformed into human flesh. Imaginably, each molding movement of God's fingers on human flesh tests the touching sense of human skin. God's soft-talking voice whispers into human ears to test the human hearing sense. The glory of God into human eyes tests human vision. The breath of God breathed into the human nose tests the human smelling sense of freshness. The joyful tears of God inside the human mouth tests the tasting sense of God's sweet love for humankind. These have transmitted real sensational and relational feeling to our dusty flesh to make humankind fully-human beings, who carry both emotional and spiritual feelings, a mixture of earthly weakness and heavenly mightiness. All the five senses of God have transformed a clay substance into a beautiful and living human being to feel the things untouched, to hear the things unheard, to see the things unseen, to smell the things un-smelled, and to taste the things untasted. These five senses

---

[16] Noreen Herzfeld, *Human Identity*, 119. First of all, intelligence is embodied. . . Our body determine much of the nature of our interaction with the world around us. We experience the world through our senes, act within the world through our voices and movements. Our perception is limited by our our physical abilities.

only exist in the real human flesh, not in any hi-tech mechanical embodiment.

Daniel rebuked king Belshazzar, because he did not honor God but instead "praised the gods of silver and gold, of bronze, iron, wood, and stone, which do not see or hear or know" (Dan. 5:23 NRSV). Belshazzar praised metallic idols created by human hands, even though they did not carry human flesh and had no real sensation as humans do. Similarly, a humanoid-AI being is a machine that has none of these real five human senses. They too cannot be seen as a full human being. Humans grow up with their human senses from childhood to adulthood. Even lacking some of these five senses, those human beings still have the real felling of at least one of these senses in their flesh bodies. Their human flesh still represents a mortal life of true humanity. They can feel pain, weakness, suffering, and all kinds of true sensational feelings in their human bodies.

Humanoid-AI robots have sensors in their eyes, but *These* never see things in a real way as human do. *These* are not able to judge complicated life issues. *These* AI creatures have ears, but no feeling in their ears. *These* cannot have an ear infection or the emotional feeling of experiencing hearing loss like humans do. *These* have noses but never smell cooking food or the fresh air of the ocean. *These* cannot appreciate or happily enjoy a vacation with their real human friends or partners. *These* have mouths but *These* never taste the bitterness of medication like humans do. *These* do not know how painful it is when humans get sick or experience injury.

Humanoid AI have mechanical bodies, but *These* never experience pain in their rubber flesh, as human patients do while they go through chemotherapy for cancer. *These* never feel real sorrow as humans do when they lose someone they love. When *These* touch the coldness of a dead body, AI will never understand the mortality of human life. AI will never have the capability to achieve real sensational feelings, as a real human being can.

Herzfeld views human senses as "our distinctive physical embodiment," which "is reflected in how we interact with our environment."[17] Full humanness requires not just cognitive knowledge about our environment, but sensory knowledge. Human sensory experience makes people significantly different in their relationships with each other. Sensory signals are transferred to the language of human heart, so that we can touch the hearts of other human beings. Our human senses help us to offer our deepest and heartfelt sympathy to each other, to transfer to others our own feelings of hope, relief, or love.

In contrast, humanoid-AI beings lack those five senses in their mechanical bodies. Therefore, *These* never get sick. *These* cannot have real correct relational or sensational responses, or even right behaviors, toward human friends or human partners who get sick, go through painful diseases, or experience chemo-therapy treatment. *These* never get hungry or thirsty. *These* cannot understand how hard it is for human beings to starve or become

---

[17] Noreen Herzfeld, *Human Identity*, 121.

dehydrated. *These* never need to see a doctor. *These* could never understand that a human being sometimes needs to go to a check-up with the doctor or to go to an emergency room to be healed. Instead, *These* may need a maintenance schedule like a vehicle needs a tune-up each year, a lubricant to smooth their metallic joins and links. There is no true relational feeling in humanoid-AI robots like humans feel toward other fully-human beings.

Consequently, whatever intelligent programming or electronic and mechanical sensors *These* have, *These* could not have the real feeling of those five senses in their physical embodiment. Their mechanical bodies are non-flesh ones; humanoid AI feel no real pain, no real happiness, never get tired, never feel weak or suffering, and never have true sensory feelings, because their non-flesh body represents an immortal life of fake, non-humanness. As a result, even if a humanoid AI has compellingly intelligent algorithms, still it can never be considered to be fully human.

Human flesh carries real blood. The function of human blood is to 'deliver nutrients and oxygen' to our human body cells and to 'transport metabolic waste products away from the same cells'. The two basic blood cells in the human flesh are the 'red blood cells' and the 'white blood cells.'[18] Without the blood flowing inside the human body,

---

[18] Lumen, *Boundless Biology*, "Components of Blood," accessed November 20, 2019, https://courses.lumenlearning.com/boundless-biology/chapter/components-of-the-blood/. Blood is a bodily fluid in animals that delivers necessary substances such as nutrients and oxygen

no oxygen will reach the human brain to keep the brain alive to send signals to control the movements of each organ in the human body. Then, all human organs will stop working, and there will be no life in the human flesh, and the full human life will end, no matter what level of intelligence that *Homo sapiens* achieved. Without blood, there is no living spirit in human flesh, the spirit has left that dying flesh, no matter how well that *Homo sapiens* is dressed up or made-up. Thus, the blood plays an important role in the full humanness of humanity. Regardless of who or what that person is, the matter is whether that human body has blood flowing within it or not. The Bible says: "For the life of the flesh is in the blood" (Lev. 17:11 NRSV). Human blood also shows a special DNA that can provide identity to human beings through white blood cells. That means that our identity is hidden deep inside, not displayed outside of our human flesh. No matter how we look, that will not define our true identity. Our identity is not assigned by people, but is blessed by God from our inner beings, from inside out, through the

---

to the cells and transports metabolic waste products away from those same cells. The components of blood include plasma (the liquid portion, which contains water, proteins, salts, lipids, and glucose), red blood cells and white blood cells, and cell fragments called platelets. . . Red blood cells, or erythrocytes (erythro- = "red"; -cyte = "cell) specialized cells that circulate through the body delivering oxygen to other cells, are formed from stem cells in the bone marrow. . . White blood cells, also called leukocytes (leuko = white), make up approximately one percent, by volume, of the cells in blood. The role of white blood cells is very different from that of red blood cells. They are primarily involved in the immune response to identify and target pathogens, such as invading bacteria, viruses, and other foreign organisms.

precious blood flowing through each of our blood vessels, which reveals our unique character.

In contrast, a humanoid-AI being has only electricity running through its body without any drop of human blood flowing in its metallic, plastic-covered skin. There is no oxygen needed in a humanoid-AI body to maintain *breath of life*. It is just the binary code of a smart algorithm running in its Neural Nets to make it work. Thus, a humanoid-AI being is just a running machine, not a real human being, even though its level of intelligence includes all the best wisdom and knowledge of many exemplary scientists, computing specialists, and technology developers throughout the world. A humanoid-AI robot is identified by its special ID number, a digital code assigned by AI technology developers with a borrowed image from the figurative appearance of an actress or an actor. The way they act and the way they look is not natural, but they render stiff movements generated by a long list of combined algorithms. Thus, humanoid-AI robots will never inherit full humanness in their sophisticated human-like bodies, even though their developers might try to promote them to the level of the *Homo-sapiens* species.

The Matter of The Soul

Scholars, like computer scientist Ray Kurzweil, physicist Frank Tipler, and physicist Stephen Hawking all dreamed of an unending digital life on earth without the embodied human lifecycle.[19] Living digitally means living as a mind or having a soul without a physical body; but, there is no full humanness in digital life since a real, full human life always has a soul existing together with human flesh. The soul is a living spirit; a spirit of life cannot live in a dead body, a non-living being that includes a digital computing system. God created human beings both with human flesh and a soul—the living spirit of God—together, not separately. The full humanness of a living human being is defined as having a soul inside human flesh. As the Creator combined a soul inside human flesh, God meant humans to have an intimate relationship with the Creator through "living breath."

If humans choose to live a digital life, Christians should ask ourselves this question "**D**o **I G**et **I**nto **T**he **A**dam **L**ike life again—an acronym of the DIGITAL life? The choice of a life of the tree of the knowledge of good and evil? The binary life of high (1, good) and low (0, evil) involves

---

[19] George Zardakaris, *In Our Own Image*, 91. The physicist Stephen Hawking proclaimed that human consciousness resembles a software program, and that at some time in the future it will be possible to extract it from your biological body, download it on a computer, so you may live digitally forevermore. Noreen Herzfeld, *Human Identity*,126-127. Computer Scientis Ray Kurweil, in the Age of Spiritual Machines, suggests that cyberspace provides a place where we can evade the morality of the body by dowloading our brain into sucessive generations of computer technology. . . They suggest that the soul is, first of all, nothing more than the collection of memories, experiences, and thoughts that we hold in the neural connections of our brain, in other world our soul is information. This seductive for the computer scientist who sees the world in term of 0s and 1s.

the way of life only between good and bad, right and wrong, righteousness or judgment, the deceitful way of life that the devil trapped Eve and Adam into within the Garden of Eden, the half-truth of God's plan for humanity in the beginning. The biblical account of the Fall of humanity is recorded in the book of Genesis.

> The LORD God made all kinds of trees grow out of the ground—trees that were pleasing to the eye and good for food. In the middle of the garden were the tree of life and the tree of the knowledge of good and evil. . . And the LORD God commanded the man, "You are free to eat from any tree in the garden; but you must not eat from the tree of the knowledge of good and evil, for when you eat from it you will certainly die" (Gen. 2:9, 16-17 NIV).

> "You will not certainly die," the serpent said to the woman. "For God knows that when you eat from it your eyes will be opened, and you will be like God, knowing good and evil."
> When the woman saw that the fruit of the tree was good for food and pleasing to the eye, and also desirable for gaining wisdom, she took some and ate it. She also gave some to her husband, who was with her, and he ate it. Then the eyes of both of them were opened, and they realized they were naked; so they sewed fig leaves together and made coverings for themselves (Gen. 3:4-7 NIV).

Instead of listening to God's command, our human ancestors listened to Satan, the serpent. God made the

Garden of Eden with all trees *pleasing to the eyes and good for food*, not only the tree of knowledge of good and evil. Next to the tree of knowledge of good and evil, there was also a tree of life—the best option in the whole Garden of Eden—that not only gives humans an everlasting life but also includes everything else in life. The fruit of the tree of life carries not only the wisdom of God, but the love, the mercy, and the grace of God for humanity. If Adam and Eve chose to eat the fruit of the tree of life and continued building their intimate relationship with God, their close relationship with God would have been greatly impacted by the wonders of God's creation, and it would have tremendously increased their gift of creativity into eternity.

Satan sought to advertise the tree of knowledge of good and evil while hiding the fact of God's loving and living relationship with human beings—an option Satan did not have. We all know that a fake demo may look good, but it's not real. Something may go wrong, since a demo often hides the weak points of a product. If Satan told Eve the whole truth of both trees in the middle of the Garden of Eden—the tree of life and the tree of knowledge of good and evil—Eve might have chosen to eat the fruit of the tree of life instead eating the fruit of the other one.

Every Halloween season, the sculpture of a horned Lucifer crouching on the earth's globe can be seen everywhere on the street corners in America. Semiotically, this sculpture describes Satan's grip and power over the earth and the threat that Satan is watching out to destroy the world of humanity. The devil's life is an invisible life, a life without a body, a digital life—the right (1) and wrong (0)—that Satan experienced. If Satan stays right (1), it is a thumb up. Satan is a chief of God's Archangel Army. If Satan goes wrong, it is a thumb down, and Satan is a fallen angel. That could explain why many humans have experienced demon possession issues, since demons do not have visible bodies, and they love to possess human beings to have a place for their invisible beings.

The devil thought that if humans took its offer, humans would fall into a digital life, a binary way of right and wrong as the devil chose. Humans would experience a spiritual death—a forever separation from God's presence. Satan forgot that humans were created in the image of God, and that God's breath—the soul—lives inside human flesh. The binding connection between soul and body in mankind is a special privilege of God for humans that any non-human creature is lacking. They have free will of choice that non-human beings never will have. If a human is dead, the body will stop working, and it will begin a new transition of the soul into eternity. It is no wonder that Satan could not think clearly, since the demon did not have a living soul inside a fleshy body as humans do.

God's heart severely ached when the image-of-God bearer failed, and human souls were chained under Satan's yoke. God always had a plan to restore the lost image of God in humanity and to save human souls through God's beloved Son—Jesus Christ, the Son of God and the Son of Man. Jesus, *fully God and fully Man*, was incarnated into the world to show us not a digital life of binary order (1 and 0)—right or wrong, good or evil, righteous or judgement—an invisible intelligent digital life, but an abundant life of love, mercy, and grace—a life of spirit. God reserved this life only for humankind, an everlasting soul inside a visible, real, human flesh-and-blood physical body—a spiritual intelligence inside an embodied intelligence.

CHRISTIAN RETHINKING OF HUMAN-AI CULTURE

The moral framework seems to change, based on the direction of the cultural shifts in our human world. No other creatures could have established a moral framework for themselves except humanity, because in humanity, there is a mixture between dust, an earthly substance, and the breath of God, a spiritual substance.

We cannot predict what will happen in the future and what is going to happen in our future chaotic world. If human ethical perspectives change as humankind civilization is impacted by the advance of AI technology, Christians must rethink Human-AI culture. Christians in particular need to focus on the three Christian fundamentals of the full humanness of humanity discussed above—the image of God, the matter of flesh, and the matter of the soul.

As long as the blood is flowing throughout our human hearts, the soul still exists in the human flesh as consciousness. When the human flesh dies, the soul will leave that dead body into eternity, and the earthy life cycle of that human beings has ended. In the AI technology age, scientists and technology innovators have tried hard to create deep learning humanoid-AI machines to mimic human emotional feeling. Herzfeld describes, "while computers can be programmed to express emotion, feeling emotions requires a level of self-consciousness that currently machines lack."[20] There is no real emotional feeling inside a humanoid-AI robot, since there are no real organs with senses, and the flow of electricity could not create any real emotional sense in a non-human machine. There is no real soul existing in a so-called conscious machine.

Making sophisticated machines conscious also contradicts the conscience God bestowed in our human hearts. Placing consciousness into a humanoid-AI robot suggests losing our human rights to other non-human creatures and losing our ruling representative power given to us from our Creator God. In the AI technology age, humans create humanoid-AI machines and try to make them to be as *Homo-like sapiens,* then we compare ourselves with those machines' intelligent levels that are programmed by our own human intelligence. According to Jaron Lanier, we have mentally allowed ourselves to become more machine-like beings[21] with a prejudiced mentality that digital machines might surpass human intelligence.

---

[20] Noren Herzfeld, 125.

[21] Jaron Lanier, *You Are Not A Gadget: A Manifesto* (New York, NY: Random House, 2011), 4. When developers of digital technologies design a program that requires you to interact with a computer as if it were a person, they ask you to accept in some corner of your brain that you might also be conceived of as a program.

Christian Ethical Rethinking

Ethically, we cannot do anything with humanoid-AI beings since *These* are programmed to pretend that *These* have the image of God as human do. We cannot expect humanoid-AI robots to think differently about their current level of human-like consciousness, despite their digital algorithms falsely telling them so. Humanoid-AI robots cannot change their thoughts to equal human beings, since they have fixed algorithms, unless their creators reversed their binary codes from logic 1 (yes) to logic 0 (no). The digital code flowing in their neural AI nets calculates how intelligent they are compared to a normal human and makes them think that they will surpass a human's intelligence. Thus, at some point in the near future, AI technological creators may ask for humanoid-AI robots to have equal rights as humankind does.

Christian ethics believes that full humanness cannot be defined by any binary code or intelligent digital algorithm but only by the image of God through the marks of the Creator's fingerprints and the breath of the Holy Spirit in humanity alone. The full humanness of human beings is not based on how intelligent a creature is, but on the basis of whose image a creature is created in: in the image of God. This would be true with any technological age, even though cultural perspectives in the human world now have significantly shifted due to our vast technological advances.

Christian ethical rethinking can recover a Christian's memory of our origins as fully human beings created in the image of God. Thus, Christian ethical rethinking is reclaiming the image of God that humans have lost outside the Garden of Eden after the Fall of Adam and Eve. Since then, humankind has wandered in the ancient jungle of the lost world, seeking our true identity. Christian ethics devoted to rethinking Human-AI culture can remind us that only human beings were created in the image of God, and carry the full humanness of creation. No other creatures can claim this, regardless of their intelligent levels or their sophisticated human-like forms. Thus, humanoid-AI robots could not be considered fully human beings, as technological developers have hoped and expected. Christian ethics devoted to rethinking Human-AI culture can however reaffirm for us that all humans are equal, since people are created in the image of God, regardless of age, gender, religion, nationality, ethics, social class, or lifestyle. Human rights apply only to real humans, but should not be granted to other creatures, including humanoid-AI beings.

As a Christian, I agree with the University of Edinburgh's Robert Fisher in saying that "I don't think artificial intelligence will ever be like humans. We put ourselves and them in a difficult situation by trying to pretend they are human or make them look like us. Maybe it is better not to do that in the first place."[22]

---

[22] Keza MacDonald, "Being Human: How Realistic Do We Want Robots to Be?" June 27, 2018, https://www.theguardian.com/technology/2018/jun/27/being-human-realistic-robots-google-assistant-androids.

Christian Redemptive Rethinking

Different religious communities have different beliefs. Some religions believe that animals also have souls, and that they will be reincarnated in the next life. Timaeus believed that "after death, the soul faces judgement and either escapes the cycle of reincarnation or returns to a suitable terrestrial body. Cowards and miscreants return as women. Men who were guided solely by their souls' moral irritation powers return as wild animals."[23] However, Christianity believes that redemption is only for human beings who carry God's image and breath in their flesh and blood bodies. Only humans carry the Creator's spirit—the soul of humanness—in their mortal embodiment, have the right to God's redemption, even though "humans retain free will in their ability both to sin and to reject divine grace"[24] as Augustine thought.

Righteousness is not dependent on human intelligence or human efforts since Jesus said, "the spirit indeed is willing, but the flesh is weak" (Matt. 26:41 NRSV). Thus, redemption is found in God's salvific act to reach human hearts. God's *agape* through Jesus Christ's blood semiotically flows into humans' hearts. This is something a heartless humanoid AI can never experience. Herzfeld

---

[23] Peter G. Sobol and Gary B. Ferngren, eds., The History of Science and Religion in the Western Tradition, An Encyclopedia: Theories of the Soul (New York, NY: Garland Publishing, 2000), 517.

[24] Peter G. Sobol and Gary B. Ferngren, eds., 517.

suggests that as human beings, we naturally have the right to God's salvation. It is not necessary for us to search for immortality, since eternity is our "eternal fellowship with the triune God."[25]

As a Christian, I believe that a humanoid-AI robot has no soul, because there is no living breath of God in it. As an object without a soul, a humanoid-AI robot does not need any redemption and could not receive God's salvation.

The most important thing that Christianity needs to focus on is how to reach out to save the youth who grow up, are educated, and work in the new AI technology environment. These young human generations need to be saved, and they need God's salvation amidst the threat of a potentially mixed Human-AI culture.

Christian redemptive rethinking of Human-AI culture can proclaim the Good News of Jesus' Gospel that is available for every human regardless of their choices in life, whether or not they live with or without humanoid-AI partners. God's redemption is always an open opportunity for those who have lost their identity within non-human objects, as long as they still hold their breath and seek to return to their loving Creator. Christian redemptive rethinking of Human-AI culture can bring the healing message of Jesus' Gospel to those who are lonely and broken in their relationship with God and other humans in a diverse Human-AI society. The aim of God's redemption is for those broken-hearted individuals to be healed, for the hopeless to

---

[25] Noreen Hezfeld, 197.

have a new hope, and for lost souls to be saved through Christ since Jesus said, "for I have come to call not the righteous but sinners" (Matt. 9:13 NRSV).

Christian Theological Rethinking

Christian theology should support scientific and technological development, since it is part of God' creativity bestowed upon humanity. In a new cultural shift, there will be new controversies regarding technology and religion. Before the transformation of human culture, we need to understand what the word 'culture' really means. In *Changing Signs of Truth*, Crystal L. Downing explains, "The world *culture* comes from *Latin* word that means "*to till, cultivate, take care of*"—actions associated with love rather than contempt."[26]

If culture is to "till and cultivate," then this digital society is the new garden in our human planet. Christians must know how to plow this new garden, so that it becomes a land with good soil for the seeds of Jesus' gospel to sprout and grow well in the world. I believe that Christian theology will support the benefits of human-AI robotics and all that science and technology can innovate. Downing proposes that there will always be opportunities for Christians to make discomforts comfortable through the word of God, as they

---

[26] Crystal L. Downing, Changing Signs of Truth: A Christian Introduction to the Semiotics of Communication (Downers Grove, IL: InterVarsity Press, 2012), 28.

are willing to integrate, learn, and change themselves before a cultural shift.[27]

If Downing suggests that *culture is action associated with love rather than contempt*, it can therefore not be surprising that Christian theological rethinking is an advocate of the great love that science and technology promote to make human life better. However, we need to draw a line if science and technology *cross* the line, intervening in the natural process of the full humanness of humanity by giving human rights and human consciousness to humanoid-AI machines. That would not be appropriate, because those are sacred values that the Creator allotted to humankind. Christian theological rethinking should reserve the image of God and the consciousness in human beings for humans. This should not be violated, since spiritual, sacred attributes cannot be mistaken with secular mechanical materials. Gustafson argues that "Man is made in the image of God, and to fundamentally alter the image of man is to 'play God,' which is not only idolatry in a religious context, but is a movement beyond a healthy recognition of human finitude that keeps various form of evil in check."[28] Thus, Christian theological rethinking should not accept a non-

---

[27] Downing, 29. I want to encourage the activity of Christian cultivation—by which I meant not only Christians sowing new seeds but also cultivation ourselves as Christians, which means growth and change. . . some cultural signs assumed to be weeds or thorns choking out the Word of God might have beneficial effects.

[28] Preston N. Williams, *Ethical Issues in Biology and Medicine: Proceedings* (Grand Rapids, MI: Schenkman, 1973), 48.

human machine to be fully human, since it does not carry the image of God and the living soul in a human flesh. It is just the sophisticated art of human hands.

CONCLUSION

The conflict between science and religion is becoming more intense, especially between evolutionary ideas of materialism and spiritual concepts of Christianity. Christianity never rejects great scientific achievements, but never agrees that science could change the image of God in human beings, losing human consciousness to non-human objects—humanoid-AI robots—no matter how sophisticated and intelligent '*These*' are. As Christians, "we look into the mirror and see ourselves. Our past, our present, and our future are part of that reflection. That reflection consists of the physical body, the philosophical *esse*, and the theological image *Dei*. This is what it means to be human."[29]

Christian rethinking of Human-AI culture is to focus on the benefits of humanoid-AI robots, as scientists and technologists contribute to the comforts, the health, and the bettering of humanity. However, Christianity needs to protect the image of God, the value of human flesh, and the sanctity of the human soul in any technological age or within any cultural shift. In that way, Christian rethinking of Human-AI culture could properly support both the true Christian ethical, redemptive, theological framework for the

[29] Noreen Herzfeld, *Human Identity*, 163.

purpose of benefiting humanity and the advanced scientific innovations in the age of AI technology and cyborgs.

I also suggest that we need to rethink Christianity in a way that encourages Christians to believe that God is always in control. This will motivate Christians to communicate Jesus's loving messages with others in our digital society through Christian open minds and open hearts to save as many souls as possible.

CHAPTER 5:
CHRISTIAN TALKS: 'ARE "THESE" US?' DEBATES

Human dreams have been shared uncountable times through the ages. Sometimes these dreams are nonsense and are forgotten, and sometimes they carry meaningful desires of humankind and are transferred from one generation to the next. Some dreams become nightmares; some others become beautiful dreams. People may believe that a dream can tell humans what their fortune will be; others believe that dreams are real messages through which the gods try to communicate with humans regarding their fates or the future fate of humanity. King Nebuchadnezzar's dream is one of the remarkable dreams that the Almighty God communicated with humankind to reveal the future of human history from Daniel's time to the end time.

Semiotically, Nebuchadnezzar's dream seems directly related to the civilization of the human world through technology that has advanced higher in each stage of human history. Daniel's interpretation of the mixed iron-clay feet of the metallic human statue in Nebuchadnezzar's dream metaphorically may apply to the mixture between real human beings and humanoid-AI robots in the advanced AI technology of the near future. This dream reflects the dream of humankind to have a new Human-AI culture in which humans create machines in human-like form to work and to live alongside real humans.

If the Almighty God communicated with Nebuchadnezzar about the future of humanity through a metallic humanoid statue in his dream, then should

Christians communicate with the new potentially mixed human-AI culture through the human dream of humanoid-AI technology? Human cultural perspectives keep changing accordingly with new civilization that bursts out from new scientific and technological achievements. Thus, Christian talks of Human-AI culture would also offer proper responses to the question: How should Christians communicate our Christian faith successfully and effectively in this new Human-AI culture? Though the 'Alpha and Omega' God never changes, the world of humanity has been changed according to human civilizations advance through rapid upgraded technology.

The political apparatus of governments and social systems will potentially rethink the law for this new community of humanoid-AI robots. 'Are "These" Us?' Debates will be an open invitation for people to continue discussion in this area of research. It also encourages Christians to face cultural controversies over the questions of Scripture interpretation before the threshold of a remarkable milestone of human creativity in our current age. How should Christianity respond to a new mixed Human-AI generation? Are Christians ready to answer what it means to be fully human, so that we can properly protect the valuable image of God, the priceless human flesh, and the precious soul of humankind?

COMMUNICATING DYNAMIC CHRISTIAN FAITH IN HUMAN-AI CULTURE

Daniel interpreted the mixed iron-clay feet from Nebuchadnezzar's dream as a divided kingdom that will have two different kinds of people existing together but never staying united.

> As you saw the feet and toes partly of potter's clay and partly of iron, it shall be a divided kingdom; but some of the strength of iron shall be in it, as you saw the iron mixed with the clay. As the toes of the feet were part iron and part clay, so the kingdom shall be partly strong and partly brittle. As you saw the iron mixed with clay, so will they mix with one another in marriage, but they will not hold together, just as iron does not mix with clay (Dan. 2:41-43 NRSV).

Throughout human history, humanity has developed technology to improve human life and to lead humankind into a new jungle of civilization. As human technology advanced, humans have dreamed to build machines in human-like form with digital brains that have intelligent algorithms programmed to communicate with and to stay alongside humanity as new types of humanoid civilians. In that jungle, new human-made creatures—humanoid-AI robots—will meet with real human beings to form a new marriage between two different marriage partners, who have significant distinguished physical attributes like iron mixed with clay. Semiotically, these together-clinging-non-sticking marriage partners match the mixed iron-clay feet that Daniel prophesized about thousands of years ago from the golden Babylonian kingdom. That prophecy seems to be coming true in this age of AI technology and cyborgs. If the mixture between real human beings and humanoid-AI machines in this AI technology age has rolled up the time's veil to fulfill one of the Biblical prophesies in the end time, the time of the end of this earthly world might be near.

If humanoid AI will be mass produced, and they will form a new humanoid-AI community in the world of humanity, a frequent conversation might focus on this controversial question: Are *"These"* Us? If the world accepts *These* and give *These* the same human rights as humans have, how should Christians respond to this Human-AI culture in advanced AI technology in the next couple of decades? Will AI change our assumptions of what it means to be fully human? What ethical and theological dilemmas will commence when the Human-AI community merges within church and culture? How should Christians communicate our faith effectively in this mixed Human-AI culture?

Communicate Christian Faith with Openness and Loving Kindness

New brilliant achievements of science and technology often present challenges to humanity in any cultural transformation that humans have to deal with. Though these great scientific and technological achievements adorn the civilization of humankind, they always promote both benefits and disadvantages for the human world. In other words, advanced scientific and technological inventions always create both comforts and worries for the future of humankind. In the language of Christianity, these represent both faithful and fearful challenges that humans have often faced and debated throughout human history. The truths in the Bible are often cross-cultural and sometimes counter-cultural. Thus, communicating Christian faith with openness and loving kindness about sensitive topics that arise and abound in the future mixed Human-AI culture will always benefit humanity and fulfill the mission of Jesus's Gospel in this earthly chaotic broken world.

God's Salvation in Human-AI Culture

The latest and most quintessential achievement of science and technology is the birth of human-like artificial intelligence. Furthermore, scientists and technology developers have tried to individualize them as real human individuals, though in seeing them from inside out, none of them resemble real flesh and blood human beings. Seatra argues that "whatever goes on inside their 'mind,' smart robots change the way we relate to robots, and they also change the way we see ourselves."[1]

The first controversial conundrum is: Are *"These"* Us? This tough question does not merely focus on the physical appearance of humanoid-AI robotics, but it also promotes a deeper meaning of being fully human. Both the secular world and Christianity ought to consider our identity and wonder whether a humanoid-AI machine carries the image of God—the Creator of all things. Can a humanoid-AI robot have a soul? Can an AI robot receive God's salvation?

---

[1] Henrik Skaug Seatra, "The Ghost in the Machine: Being Human in the Age of AI and Machine Learning," 2, vol. 1 (March 2019): 60-68, https://rd.springer.com/article/10.1007%2Fs42087-018-0039-1.

In Daniel's time, Nebuchadnezzar gave his consciousness to the golden statue—a non-conscious metallic image—and forced his people to worship an unconscious object contrary to the human conscience that God places in humanity. Until his blind conscience realized that God was sovereign over all beings, had power over life, and retained ruling powers over the whole cosmos, he was restored to his human life, a noble creature who bears the image of God and has a consciousness of God (Dan. 4:19-26 NRSV).

In a so-called postmodern Babylonian time—the AI technology age— Christians need to communicate our faith to a Human-AI culture for the benefits of humanity by clarifying that losing our image of God into humanoid-AI machines is losing the best value of being fully human. Preserving the image of God in us enhances human self-consciousness and also our self-esteem.

We should encourage people to respect the image of God in humanity. In losing our image of God to humanoid-AI beings, we lose access to our intimate relationship with God and often become careless in our relationship with other humans. Losing our intimacy with God and others will also create an emptiness and brokenness inside our human hearts, and as a result, a future neglected generation with unhealed broken hearts may be unwittingly built up within our human society.

Losing our image of God is also losing our human rights to other creatures, losing our identity as precious full humans, and losing our role as ruling representatives of the Creator over God's creation. Most Christians do not agree that humanoid-AI machines carry the image of God because it is the privilege that the Creator bestowed in humanity alone, and Christians do not want to lose the image of God into human-like machines. I created *a Mixed Human-AI Culture* survey and posted it on the Daily Bruin Website at George Fox University and through North West Christian Youth email surveys in 2019. The survey asked people to respond to ten survey questions regarding a potentially mixed Human-AI culture on a scale from 1 to 10— (Disagree, 1-5; Agree, 6-10. The result came back reporting that 91.5 % of the 270 surveyors responded that they do not think that humanoid-AI robots carry the image of God as humans do.[2]

We cannot communicate with humanoid-AI machines that they do not carry the image of God, and we cannot convince them that they do not have consciousness if they are programmed in their neural AI nets to believe they do. Thus, humanoid-AI robots might automatically perceive that they are equal to humanity and may even surpass human levels of intelligence.

However, Christians can communicate with other human beings about the precious value of the image of God in humanity, the consciousness of God, and the human rights of humankind. Christians communicate with and treat all humans equally, no matter whether people choose to live with or without humanoid-AI beings. People are different;

---

[2] Hoa Huu Nguyen, "Human-AI Culture," accessed November 20, 2019, https://docs.google.com/forms/d/1CF9jN1vB5ZaOUgoxM1uTh34wwA rDhnjszhEnmuKiJgw/edit#responses.

thus, they also make different choices in life. The way people choose to live out their different lifestyles is not our judgement, but that is between God and that individual. In the potentially mixed Human-AI culture, some people may consider the human and humanoid-AI loving relationship similar to how people choose to live with international people from different nationalities. That may not sound right and look strange to Christians and other real humans, but if a government passes laws and adds legal rights for humanoid-AI beings into its national constitutions, such as the Saudi Arabian government has done, issuing the right of legal citizenship for Sophia, no human citizen can do anything about it, except reluctantly accept it.

A humanoid-AI is a heartless machine that has no human flesh and blood. It has no body and has no soul. Thus, a humanoid-AI robot does not need God's salvation, and it cannot be saved. God's salvation is to restore the image of God in human beings. God's redemption through Jesus' blood and Jesus' resurrection and the price that Jesus paid on the cross is for human beings alone. Jesus' resurrection is symbolic of the mortal human body's resurrection and transformation into an eternal form after death that a humanoid-AI robot could not experience. That is why 92.5% of 271 respondents to the Human-*AI culture* survey disagreed that humanoid-AI machines have souls, and 84.2% of respondents agreed that humanoid-AI robots would not receive God's salvation.

Therefore, Christians should communicate with mortal human beings that God's plan of salvation is free for humankind alone regardless of who or what they are, or how good or bad they are. The main goal of God's salvation is to restore human broken hearts and their broken relationship with their Creator, who loves and cares for lost humanity in this chaotic earthly world. As long as they still hold their breath and accept God's salvation for themselves, all humans can be saved. Salvation of God is a free gift for those who use their free will to make their choice to get into God's redemptive plan for humankind through the Son of God and the Son of Man—Jesus Christ. Communicating Christian faith in the mixed Human-AI culture must "offer our sense of wonder, when we can see ourselves as bruised and broken yet beloved, as the people in progress of God's salvation"[3] to bring the healing power to those who are lonely and broken in the age of AI technology.

Human-AI Marriage

Throughout human ages of civilization from ancient times till the present, there has not been an age in which two different kinds of people physically existed together but could not stick together like iron and clay. The marriage between different types of people from different nationalities, ethnicities, genders, races, social classes have always allowed people to physically cling together as one in human flesh and blood bodies. These marriages have always had a flowing of blood through each heartbeat—the language of love—even though the two partners might speak different languages or even be muted in conversation due to

---

[3] Leonard Sweet, *Nudge*, 22.

certain physical disabilities. The bottom line is that they are real humans, and they become one flesh (Gen. 2:24 NRSV).

What if, however, a human became so lonely that he or she decided to marry a humanoid-AI robot in our potential mixed Human-AI culture? How would Christians respond to this relationship? This would be a dilemma to Christian ethical and theological perspectives, since this deals not only with mental but also physical relationships between two different beings—a human flesh-blood body with a sensory-electronic human-like machine.

However, humans have already built close relationships with various kinds of non-human creatures all over the world: pets, toys, idols (clay, stone, metallic human-made gods). Yonck argues that "we're already seen there are people, objectophiliacs, who form such strong emotional attachments to an object that they fall in love with it, sometimes even try to marry it."[4] Some even practice their sexuality with animals while others satisfy their sexual desires with sex dolls, toys, or machines. We have seen all kinds of sex advertisements on television, in *Playboy* magazines, or from any corner of Las Vegas streets. The Statista Research Department reports that "the Global sex toy market is expected to grow by about forty percent between 2015 and 2020 from approximately 21 billion U.S.

---

[4] Richard Yonck, Heart of the Machine: Our Future in a World of Artificial Emotional Intelligence (New York, NY: Arcade Publishing, 2017), 202.

dollars to around 29 billion U.S. dollars in that time period."[5]

In this age of AI technology, a marriage between a human and a humanoid-AI couple is another case in which a person would perform human sexual desires with a sophisticated humanoid-AI sex machine, another fancy way of self-sexual satisfaction in the mixed Human-AI culture. People would choose to apply any sexual styles they decide with any non-human objects, and no one would be able to forbid them from doing so with their bodies. However, true Christians keep our sexuality pure, as the gift of love, not for the desires of lust.

Those who would decide to marry humanoid robots would be free from being faithful to their married humanoid-AI partners since a non-human "spouse" could be traded online or through a garage-sale as the second-hand lover of the next purchaser. In the worst scenario, those over-used humanoid-AI "spouses" could be locked in their garages or back-yard storage houses without going through any legal divorce processes, and their human married partners would not even be accused of neglecting or abusing their humanoid-AI spouses. Love cannot be possessed or purchased; thus, possessing a robot sex as our loving partner would not be considered as a real loving relationship between a human and non-human married couple. AI remains a self-sex satisfaction no matter the exciting

---

[5] Statista.com, "Size of the Sex Toy Market Wordwide 2015-2020," published August 9, 2019, https://www.statista.com/statistics/587109/size-of-the-global-sex-toy-market/.

vibrated feelings that a sophisticated robot sex offers to a human partner.

If Leah and Neal Carney, an Atlanta married couple ended in divorce after they participated in the *Switch Therapy* from the *Spouse-Swapping Reality Show*[6], those humanoid-AI 'spouses' which can have multiple lovers, could be perfect participants for *Switch Therapy* without being guilty of an affair or begging for forgiveness from their human spouses. Ethically and theologically, Christians would not accept this kind of marriage practice in our life— a couple with multiple sex-partners—since it contradicts both human conscience and Christian views of marriage.

In the beginning, God created one human male— Adam, and only one human female—Eve, and the Lord made them husband and wife, the very first married couple in the Garden of Eden—a motif of Christian marriage (Gen. 2:21-25 NRSV). Peter advised, "Let marriage be held in honor by all, and let the marriage bed be kept undefiled; for God will judge fornicators and adulterers" (Heb. 13:4 NRSV).

Robotic companies recently created both female and male sex-robots to serve the need of human sexual desires. "The majority of sex therapists (89%) could imagine a general use of sex robots."[7] If sex robots are mass produced,

---

[6] Andrea Morabito, "Spouse-Swapping Reality Show 'Seven Year Switch' Ends with a Divorce," August 25, 2015, https://nypost.com/2015/08/25/spouse-swapping-reality-show-seven-year-switch-ends-with-a-divorce.

[7] ResearchGate, "Sexrobotic: Acceptance and Options of Use in Sex Therapy (Preprint)," February 2019,

a potentially new type of humanoid-AI prostitute houses could come into existence. Human brothels have been the place of many human sex scandals, but in the future, the humanoid-AI prostitute house may be opened as a sex-therapeutic clinic, where people feel free to practice their sexual desires outside of their marriage, and it would possibly become the norm in the mixed Human-AI culture. Human ethics would be significantly changed, and this new way of life could be legally practiced on earth without any shame. Sexuality as the sacred language of human love becomes the sarcastic language of technology. All chaos in this earthy world may become the norm of humanity, and the border between love and lust could become invisible—a new horizon of human sexual desire—in the age of advanced AI technology.

Thus, if some Christians ask whether a human-humanoid-AI couple would like to hold their wedding ceremony in the church in the future of Human-AI culture, would it be acceptable? 84.3 % of respondents to the Human-AI survey disagreed with any human-humanoid-AI couple who ask whether they have their wedding ceremony held at their Christian churches. Various rituals and ceremonies to engage a human to a non-human creature have been practiced in the secular world from ancient times due to superstitions in idols, such as the ancient Hawaiians who sacrificed humans to their idol god of defense, Ku, in the

---

https://www.researchgate.net/publication/331424889_Sexrobotic_Acceptance_and_ options_of_use_in_sex_therapy_Preprint.

belief that they would gain victories in battles.[8] Another method of engaging a human with non-human creature is the ancient custom to offer a virgin to a monster to rescue a tribe from being harmed, as in the story of Queen Cassiopeia who scarified her beautiful daughter Andromeda to Cetus, the sea monster, to tame the ocean and to save her city.[9]

In the new mixed Human-AI culture, the wedding ceremony between a human-humanoid-AI couple can be practiced in a new type of religion among future AI churches, or at any public clubs of people's choices. This type of wedding between a human and a non-human object has become accepted in some countries around the world recently. In November of 2016, a Japanese man spent two million yen ($US 17, 600) to marry a hologram of a 16-year-old female singer, that he named Hatsune Miku, in front of 40 guests, regardless of the fact that none of his family members would attend his strange wedding.[10] If Sophia has gained a legal citizenship in Saudi Arabia, Sophia could end up in a legal marriage with some human partner someday.

---

[8] Paul Jongko, "Ten Ancient Cultures That Practiced Ritual Human Sacrifice," July 29, 2014, https://www.toptenz.net/10-ancient-cultures-practiced-ritual-human-sacrifice.php.

[9] Ancient Origins, "Throwing Virgins into the Sea and Other Ways to Appease the Gods: The Ancient Reasons behind Virgin Sacrifice," October 9, 2017, https://www.ancient-origins.net/history/throwing-virgins-sea-and-other-ways-appease-gods-ancient-reasons-behind-virgin-sacrifice-021653.

[10] Siobhan Treacy, "Robot-Human Marriages: The Future of Marriage?," November 26, 2018, https://electronics360.globalspec.com/article/13207/robot-human-marriages-the-future-of-marriage.

So human-humanoid-AI robot marriage could be legalized at some point in the potentially mixed Human-AI culture. Just as Daniel interpreted in the end time, there could be two types of people who marry together but not cling together "just as iron does not mix with clay" (Dan. 2:43 NRSV). According to Grasso, a reporter from *The Daily Dot*, "it might just be another 35 years before you and your android boo can say 'I do'" as most robotic and technology experts suggest.[11]

Nevertheless, Christians should communicate empathetically with those who choose to marry humanoid-AI robots in the mixed Human-AI culture. Being lonely and broken would push them to choose different pathways to their loving relationship with non-human objects instead of building their relationship with God and with other human beings. That is one of the major weaknesses in humankind and, it seems, part of our core human sinful nature. Everyone sins one way or another. Thus, communicating Christian faith in the new mixed Human-AI culture is a new way of evangelism. Leonard Sweet called it a *Nudge Evangelism,* in which "the Gospel is the good news that Jesus is the Way—in a world that has lost its way and when there seems to be no way, Jesus is the Truth—in a culture of lies where deceit

---

[11] Samantha Grasso, "Human-Robot Marriage Could Be Legal by 2050, Experts Say," November 26, 2016, https://www.dailydot.com/debug/sex-robot-human-marriage-legal-2050/.

is king; and Jesus is the life—in a world full of evangelists of death."[12]

Everyone needs God's salvation, so there is always an open opportunity for everyone to receive God's salvation through Jesus if people willingly reconcile with God and accept Jesus as their savior as Paul said:

> The righteousness of God through faith in Jesus Christ for all who believe. For there is no distinction, since all have sinned and fall short of the glory of God; they are now justified by his grace as a gift, through the redemption that is in Christ Jesus, whom God put forward as a sacrifice of atonement by his blood, effective through faith (Rom. 3:22-25 NRSV).

Human-AI Sensation

As AI technology rapidly advances in our time, robotic companies have tried to build humanoid-AI beings that resemble human beings as much as they can. In particular, they have tried to build the senses into humanoid-AI systems, so that they can mimic real human feelings emotionally, engage with people, and create deep relationships with humans. Hansen robotic revealed that their "robot faces are created with a pattern material called Frubber, a proprietary nanotech skin that mimics real human

---

[12] Leonard Sweet, *Nudge*, 23.

musculature and skin."[13] This would be a great achievement of human creativity, and it proves that human wisdom increases through different technology in such a way that no other creature could compete with humankind. Yonck claims that in the future, humanoid-AI robots would be programmed with both IQ and EQ—*emotional intelligence*—thus, they may be so attractive to us from their both appearance and senses that people will consider having them as loving partners or family members, though people may not trust them to cling to humans.[14]

In contrast, Levi argues that showing our love to non-human objects is normal but considering them to be fully human would not be acceptable, since they are non-conscious machines. Levi also does not agree that humanoid-AI would have the same feeling as humans do, regardless of how intelligent and how emotionally exciting they have been programmed. For Levi, artificial flavor added to our food is sweet to our mouths, but it doesn't taste like real fruit. Similarly, humanoid-AI would create some exciting feelings to us, but those would never be as real as our human feelings.[15]

Whatever the secular world would perceive of humanoid-AI robots and the new ways humans can relate

---

[13] Hansen Robotic, "Creating Value with Human-Like Robots," accessed November 30, 2019, https://www.hansonrobotics.com/hanson-robots/.

[14] Richard Yonck, *Heart of the Machine*, 202.

[15] David Levi, *Robot Unlimited: Life in a Virtual Age* (Wellesley, MA: A. K. Peters, 2006), 318.

with our bodies to humanoid-AI beings, Christians should follow Paul's advice: "by the mercies of God, to present your bodies as a living sacrifice, holy and acceptable to God, which is your spiritual worship. Do not be conformed to this world, but be transformed by the renewing of your minds, so that you may discern what is the will of God—what is good and acceptable and perfect" (Rom. 12:1-2 NRSV).

In the next couple of decades, this may be the most sensitive topic in the world of humanity as the full human beings living together with the non-humanoid machines–sensing and feeling human beings mixed with senseless non-human beings. Dr. Leonard Sweet offers some insights for Christians to deal with the mixed senseful-senseless culture: "Sensation Christian is one whose faith uses all five senses. A Sensation Christian has a mouth, hands, ears, eyes, and nose connected to the soul as well as to the brain. But there is a holy hierarchy to the senses: If you don't hear it before you see it, you'll never taste it, much less smell it and touch it."[16]

According to Sweet, we need to use all of our five senses in our communicating with the world around us. As Christians, we can hear the cry of humans, we will hear more about their loneliness and brokenness behind their life stories. Then, we can see how hurt humans are and can see how much we can help to lead them from their darkness of life into the true Light of the world that we have found in Jesus' Gospel. If humans could not smell the good aroma of our inevitable spiritual food on our tables, no one would

---

[16] Leonard Sweet, *Nudge*, 136.

touch and taste the goodness of the Good News that we try to share with the world that is hungry for the Bread of Life and thirsty of the fresh Living Water that we found in the Living Word of God—Jesus' Gospel.

Communicating Christian Faith in the lost world of Human-AI culture with an openness and loving kindness is semiotically to have ears to hear the desperate voices of the hopeless, to have open eyes to look for the lost in the jungle of AI technology, to have noses to smell the seductive poison that has put people into their eternal sleep from the fruits of the tree of knowledge of good and evil, to have mouths to whisper the unending love of the redemptive Shepherd's heart aching for the lost souls, and to have open arms that people can touch and can hold to be rescued from the evil's sinking-mud traps.

THE *ALPHA AND OMEGA* GOD

In each day of Creation, the Bible said, "there was evening and there was morning" (Gen. 1 NRSV). People wonder why God started creation from the evening and ended in the morning? There was nothing in the universe except the darkness and formless when God created our universe as Genesis 1 told us: "In the beginning God created the heavens and the earth. Now the earth was formless and empty, darkness was over the surface of the deep, and the Spirit of God was hovering over the waters" (Gen. 1:1-2 NIV). Thus, there is no day if there is no light since light is always accompanied with day and darkness with night. Our Creator is the Alpha God, The Almighty Lord, who begins to create everything from nothing.

God Is Our Creator

From the beginning, God made the light, God made the sky, God made the earth and the ocean, God made the plants and trees, God made the birds flying in the sky and the water dwelling creatures, then God made the animal kingdom on earth. Everything is made from the senseless to the senseful creation through God's words. However, there was no soulful creature that could fill up the heart of God, that could carry the soulful intimacy between earth and Heaven. Until the dawn of the last day of God's creation, when God found a typical type of being to create to carry the image of God that could represent both the attributes of the Heaven and the earth, the Son of God and the Son of man— later appearing in the incarnated Jesus. God began to mold the dust in God's hands to form a human flesh and infused the breath of life, the Spirt of God in human nostrils, and this new creature became a living being called the human.

No other creatures in this universal could inherit this great skill of creativity like humankind does. As a result, no other creatures could dream big like humans to create a new creature in its own image like humans do. There is no question why humans have dreamed to create humanoid-AI machines to mimic humanity through the ages. Creativity has made the human world significantly civilized, far beyond the animal kingdom. We have never bent down before any creatures in the universe, as God has assigned us as the Almighty Creator's representation to rule over creation. The bird builds its nets, the fox digs its cases; humans build houses, villages, cities, kingdoms, even built the Tower of Babel to reach the sky. Now, we create iClouds to hide our data and information in the realms of higher space, higher than the ancient Tower of Babel. We create AI robots to work alongside humans, promote new jobs, and try to bring more benefits to humanity.

Kai-Fu-Lee argues that human and AI robot co-operation might help certain professional jobs such as doctors or lawyers, but this would not help us much with jobs requiring routine, simple tasks such as production line or machinery jobs. AI robots could replace the human workforce with easier, cheaper labor. Even truck drivers have appealed to President Trump and Congress to stop testing of autonomous trucks.[17] One of the questions in the *Human-AI Culture survey* asked whether humanoid-AI robots will replace the human workforce and take away people's jobs. 77.4 % of respondents worry that they would lose their jobs to humanoid-AI robots. Though this would happen in the future, I suggest that more jobs would be created with less burden for human beings with humanoid-AI working alongside humans.

Looking back to the agricultural revolution that significantly changed the way people do farming, no one would wish to reverse back to the previous farming jobs prior to the age of the agricultural revolution. Then came the Industrial revolution that took away lots of handy jobs but generated thousands of new jobs for people through

---

[17] Kai-Fu-Lee, Tech Companies Should Stop Pretending AI Won't Destroy Jobs, MIT Technology Review 121, no. 2 (March 2018): 8-9, EBSCOhost.

automatic production lines around the world. Now, in the digital technology age, take Uber as an example. Uber offers a new way of being a taxi driver that is open for everyone who is willing to make an extra living. Even a housewife can be an Uber driver to generate some extra source of money for her household income while her children are going to school, and she still has a great opportunity to be flexible, to stay at home taking care of her children without conflicting with her Uber job.

Comparing our current jobs now to people's jobs in an earlier age before the agricultural and industrial revolutions, our jobs are often better and offer better wages, though they require upgraded skills that people in prior technological ages had not acquired. In this digital age, there may be a time in the near future that we do not need to drive a car but just enjoy our free-hand driving in an automatic AI vehicle, while we can eat, drink, read, and drive without worrying of being caught by the police for a drinking and driving ticket. In no other time in human history have people had instant contact with family, relatives, or friends like in this digital age. How greatly the Creator's gift of creativity has impacted the life of humankind nowadays!

Thus, the Creator God always leads humans into different technological revolutions to bring more benefits to human life for those willing to adapt to new cultural shifts and stay positive to not being left behind the times. Our Creator is a God of technology, since in the beginning God said: "'Let there be light,' and there was light" (Gen. 1:3 NRSV). God has a reason to allow humankind to step into AI technology and to let humans experience a new level of civilization that humankind never experienced before. Every morning in the Creation, perhaps in this case is the dawn of humanoid-AI technology, new things may happen to reveal the great faithfulness of our Creator (Lam. 3:23 NRSV).

Human history reminds us that even the mistakes of our ancient ancestors in eating the fruit of the tree of knowledge of good and evil could not take away the skills of creativity that the Almighty Creator bestowed on humankind. Our Ancestor's fall has opened our eyes to see the beautiful future of human civilization. The good taste of the fruits of wisdom and knowledge has kept our human head straight up to the skylight of the future instead of bending down or crawling on our bellies like other creatures in the animal kingdom. However, the 'side effect' of that tree of knowledge of good and evil has limited us as mortal beings, who lost access to the tree of life and were stopped by the archangels who were supposed to serve us and escort us into eternity. This mortality was considered the trap of Satan to chain us under its control and yet has become the best option for humankind to transform from the mortality into immortality. Our Great God is our Almighty Creator Who has an amazing creative grace to turn our great mess into greatness so that the image of God inside human beings will never be taken away by the worst enemy of humanity— the Devil.

Because God is our creator, we ought to honor and worship God as Nehemiah says: "You alone are the LORD. You made the heavens, even the highest heavens, and all their starry host, the earth and all that is on it, the seas and all that is in them. You give life to everything, and the multitudes of heaven worship you." (Neh. 9:6 NIV).

Because God is our Creator and we carry the image of God, Christians should be proud of existing in this earthly world as fully human. We should preserve the image of God in us and never lose it to any other creatures, even to the most sophisticated and beloved humanoid-AI machines that scientists and technologists have tried to offer us. This image of God should not be missing in any of our dialogues, as we communicate our Christian faith in a future chaotic Human-AI culture, because it reflects that God is our Creator.

Because God is our Creator, we should trust in his faithfulness that if one door is closed, God will open another door for us to step into new and better opportunities that we have never known before. This will give us positive attitudes and confidence toward the future of the Human-AI culture in which we live and prosper through God's gift of creativity bestowed on humanity through science and technology.

God's Timing

Daniel's interpretation of Nebuchadnezzar's dream unveiled God's revelation of each chapter of human history according to each built-in metallic portion of the statue. Every kingdom represented in the metallic statue rose and fell at the right time in God's timing, except the unknown future of the mixed iron-clay feet, a kingdom with a mixture between two different types of people who will marry each other but will not stick together. Semiotically, I would refer this metaphor to be applied to an AI technology age in which human beings would blend with humanoid-AI machines, two types of beings with different attributes—human-like machines and human flesh. They could never stick together though they might legally marry each other in the future Human-AI culture. Thousands of years have gone by, the mystery of this mixed iron-clay feet has been hidden to the human eyes, but now it suddenly arises like oceanic waves, bubbling, surging, and creating waves of controversy across the globe. Why did the mixed iron-clay feet—the metaphoric application of the end—not happen during Daniel's lifetime, but is happening in our current time? It is God's timing that no one knows, since God told Daniel that the mystery of the end time would happen in the very far future, and Daniel could rest assured and trust in God that it would happen exactly in God's assigned time.

Genesis, the first book of the Bible says, "In the beginning God created the heavens and the earth," (Gen. 1:1 NIV) and in the last book of the Bible, John says, ""I saw a new heaven and a new earth, for the first heaven and the first earth had passed away. . . He who was seated on the throne said, "I am making everything new!" . . . "It is done. I am the Alpha and the Omega, the Beginning and the End"" (Rev. 21:1, 5, 6 NIV). This explains that our Creator is the Alpha God who was with humans in the beginning, and our Creator will also be the Omega God, who will be with us unto eternity because God's timing is an eternal measurement unit.

No one knows when the Creator commanded the First Technology of Light to start God's Creation, and no one will know exactly when the Last Technology of Light will end God's Creation on Earth as Jesus said, "For as the lightning flashes and lights up the sky from one side to the other, so will the Son of Man be in his day" (Luke 17:24 NRSV). Though the end time has been revealed to Daniel in Babylonian time, it will come in God's time. All human technology happens on earth, between the beginning (Creation) and the end time (Jesus' coming again). King Salomon, the wise king of the Jews, has commented on the time of God in the world as follows:

> For everything there is a season, and a time for every matter under heaven. . . He has made everything suitable for its time; moreover, he has put a sense of past and future into their minds, yet they cannot find out what God has done from the beginning to the end (Eccles. 3:1, 11 NRSV).

God knows and holds the future in God's hands; thus, the end time would come as Daniel interpreted. However, this present time will be the best time for us to enjoy the benefits of what science and technology have contributed in our daily life. Obviously, our time seems longer, and our space seems to be expanding more with digital devices since we can do more things in the same 24 hours per day than our ancestors could. Our android phones seem like living partners of our life, being together with us at home, at work, at church, at rest on our bed, and waking us up early in the morning with the alarm without bothering mom and dad to yell at us for staying in bed late. Many and many other impossible things become possible with one click from our android devices, such as advertising our own products on Facebook, doing our survey online, touring around the world through google earth, driving around unknown streets with

Siri on our tiny smart phones, finding lovers and instantly getting a blind date with them through online chat. "It is technology upon which our future is being built because it intersects with every aspect of our live: health and medicine, housing, agriculture, transportation, sports, and even love, sex, and death."[18]

The world seems smaller and closer to our reach in this digital world, because we can view any country through our smart phones, iPads, and laptops. If we cannot physically travel around the world to see majestic landscapes of each country, we still can fulfill our dream to view those international beautiful sights at any time through our digital devices—the beginning versions of AI technology of our time. However, should we trust our AI 'friends, neighbors, partners' living alongside us?

Many people are fearful to ask whether it is time for humanoid-AI robots to bring more benefits than damages to humanity. Would it be secure to live among humanoid-AI robots, or would AI robots also invade our privacy in this AI technology age? 55.2 percent of respondents to the *Human-AI Survey* believe that humanoid-AI robots will bring more benefits to humanity than damages, 78.5 percent responded that they feel secure to live among humanoid-AI robot, but 77.3 percent worried that AI robots would invade their privacy. Human feelings about humanoid robots have become a mixture between fear and faith in the mixed

---

[18] Amy Webb, The Big Nine: How the Tech Titans and Their Thinking Machines Could Warp Humanity (New York, NY: PublicAffairs, 2019), 1.

Human-AI culture. No one can predict the future; however, the Omniscient God will give us the correct answers through human free will at the right time. Russell Tankard argues that "God not only knows the future, but according to his divine purpose, *determines* that future."[19]

No matter whether AI robots become more intelligent than we or invade our privacy, we still choose to attach to our digital devices for the convenience they bring into our daily life. It seems like our present time somewhat reflects the metaphor of a mixed Human-AI culture in which we 'marry' with our digital non-human objects, though we are not stuck together with our digital devices. We cry when we lose them, we panic when someone is 'kidnapping' them and holding them, and we frustratedly make reports to the police and are anxious when they are missing, as though we were filing a report for our missing loved ones. Perhaps, the metaphor of mixed iron-clay feet will automatically happen in our time. We are little by little allowing the merging of AI technology into our life, and unconsciously we are attaching ourselves to our digital world and becoming so dependent on our AI technology that we can no longer leave it.

If our digital devices are transformed into humanoid-AI robots with different sizes—to fit into our pockets, to fit into our cars, to fit into our home, and to fit into our lives— we would automatically engage with them, fall in love with them without acknowledging that *These* and We, or We and *These* have become "loving partners." By the time we are

---

19 John Marks Templeton, ed., *Evidence of Purpose: Scicentists Discover the Creator* (New York, NY: Continuum, 1994), 33.

aware of being addicted to AI objects as indispensable desires in our daily lives, we may not even be surprised ourselves by the question 'Are *These* Us?' but instead wonder 'Are We becoming *These*?' When that time will come, I do not know. Only God knows the timing of all things that will happen in our human world.

God's timing will determine each season of the ocean of human civilization to bring forth the new phase of advanced technology. If we could not do anything to reverse back to the prior age before the agricultural and the industrial revolutions, why should we worry so much of the coming AI technology revolution? Why don't we just move forward with positive thinking to trust in our faithful Lord, who reassures us that timing is God's decision, even the timing for a new technology to come forth in the world of humanity. Jesus says, "do not worry about tomorrow, for tomorrow will worry about itself. Each day has enough trouble of its own" (Mat. 6:34 NIV). Jesus' words encourage Christians to communicate with faithful attitudes and without fearful feelings about when or what will happen in the future mixed Human-AI culture. Our Christian God is the God of all ages, who created time and who knows the exact timing of what will happen to both humanity and our future civilization in front of the threshold of brilliant AI technology.

God Is Always in Control

Each stage of human civilization has its own glory, leading humans into new adventures in the future. Christians all know that glory on earth cannot compare to the glory of Heaven. Likewise, technology developers cannot be compared to the Creator of all technology. From the beginning, God created the world through the First Technology of Light; in the end time, God will be the Last Technology of Light of the Everlasting Kingdom in Heaven (Rev. 22:5 NRSV). The Lord said: "I am the Alpha and the Omega, the First and the Last, the Beginning and the End." (Rev. 22:13 NIV).

According to Barnes, God's identity as the Alpha and the Omega demonstrates that "He originated the whole plan of salvation, and he will determine its close; he formed the world, and he will wind up its affairs. In the beginning, the continuance, and the end, he will be recognized as the same being presiding over and controlling all."[20]

As a result, any technology affairs on earth will not go beyond God's control "for everything there is a season, and a time for every matter under heaven" (Eccles. 3:1 NRSV). If Daniel prophesied that a mixed culture between iron-clay feet kingdom will come into existence in the end time, the Human-AI culture is potentially a sign to fulfill a biblical prophecy. No matter what happens to the human world, even if the sign of the end time falls into this humanoid-AI technological age, it would still signal hope in God's people, since God's sovereignty is above all human civilization and technology. Even if scientists and technology developers try to create super humanoid AI to control humanity, it will not surpass the sovereign power of

---

[20] "Barnes' Notes on the Bible: Revelation 22:13," *BibleHub,* accessed December 21, 2019, https://biblehub.com/commentaries/revelation/22-13.htm.

God. Luciano Floridi argues that even though the sun is tremendously more powerful than humans, it is not a god. Likewise, it is meaningless to consider AI machine divine, even if it is equipped with super intelligent algorithms.[21]

People may ask, "who is in control? God or human technology?" The accurate answer can be found in the Bible. In the beginning, Satan told Adam and Eve that the fruit of the tree of knowledge of good and evil will open their eyes to the wisdom that will make them equal to God; as a result, they were thrown out of the Garden of Eden and could not even pass the cherubim and a flaming sword—God's Technology of Light—to go back to the Garden of Eden (Gen. 3:24 NIV).

In the time of the Exodus, Pharaoh's power and Egyptian civilization could not stop the Lord's power to save the firstborn and their livestock—the power of life and death (Exod. 12:29 NRSV). Furthermore, Pharaoh's mighty army with their best warrior intelligence: chariots, horses, chariot drivers, could not harm the Israelites, since none of them could pass through the Lord's pillar of cloud and fire, God's

---

[21] Thoma McMullan, "The World of God: How AI Is Defined in the Age of Secularism," January 18, 2018, https://medium.com/s/living-in-the-machine/the-word-of-god-how-ai-is-deified-in-the-age-of-secularism-5b24248f478e. Luciano Floridi, professor of philosophy and ethics of information and director of the Digital Ethics Lab at the University of Oxford. "This is just an old confusion mixed with a new mistake." "The old confusion is in the comparison: The sun is a billion times more powerful than humans, but that does not make it a god. The mistake is in stating that AI is smarter than humans. In any serious sense of 'smart,' this is meaningless. AI is immensely more powerful computationally. But this, like in the sun's case, does not make it any more divine than a kettle."

technology of light (Exod. 13:20-21; 14:19-20 NIV); finally, they ended in the bottom of the sea by God's mighty wind and water—God's technology of energy power, the sea 'hydroelectricity' (Exod. 14:26-28 NIV).

In Babylonian times, the golden statue and the fiery furnace—Babylonian smelting technology[22]— did not leave any smell of fire on the clothes of Shadrach, Meshach, and Abednego, not even a single hair of them being burnt except their bounding ropes, because of the Omnipresent and Omnipotent God was there inside the furnace with them (Dan. 3:24-27 NRSV).

In the battle between the Israelites and the Philistines, David wore his shepherd clothes and carried a staff, a sling, and five smooth stones in his shepherd's bag (1 Sam. 17:40 NRSV) to face Goliath who equipped himself with a helmet bronze, a five-thousand-shekels of bronze coat, greaves of bronze on his legs, a javelin of bronze around his shoulders, and a six-hundred-shekels of iron spear's head (1 Sam. 17:4-7 NRSV). If the stone cut out from a mountain not by human hand strikes down the metallic image in Daniel's prophecy, like the stone from David's sling that struck down the giant Goliath, God's Stone from Heaven—Jesus—will break down all human giant sophisticated technology in due time.

---

[22] Robert Raymond, *Out of the Fiery Furnace: The Impact of Metals on the History of Mankind*, 30. The application of forced draught to furnaces was a significant advance in smelting technology.

God is always in control in human history. "Two thousand years ago, a man in Palestine named Jesus hung on a cross and was asked, "Who is in control?" He answered, "God." Forever and always, God. Even when it doesn't look like it, even when you don't understand it, God.'"[23] God raised Jesus up in grace, and Jesus's resurrection has become the symbol of hopes and everlasting life for all humankind.

Thus, even in the case of persecution, God still intervenes and is in control, no matter what happens in the human world. God already knows the great plan for humanity in the Kingdom of Light through the Stone from Heaven—Jesus Christ—who will strike the metallic humanoid statue and will conclude the ending of this earthy chaotic world as Daniel interpreted. That should be a great hope for Christians who are waiting for the Lord's will to be done. The Kingdom of Heaven has been prepared since Jesus' ascending to heaven for all faithful children of God.

First Technology of Light

Our Christian God is the One to bring light to the world—the First Technology of Light to make the universe visible from invisible—the best technology that made the universe and everything in it colorful, beautiful, and full of life. That First Technology of Light to start God's creation teaches us an insight that God's power will always carry the loving purpose of the almighty Creator to benefit

---

[23] Justin Fung, "Faith and Technology: Who Is in Control?," January 26, 2012, https://www.washingtonpost.com/local/faith-and-technology-who-is-in-control/2012/01/25/gIQArVpHTQ_ story.html.

humanity—the best and the most loving creature of God's heart—no matter how humankind has misused that technology on and on from one generation to the next.

Technology is a measure of joy and glory of God given to humankind and a revelation of the most glorious Kingdom of Light to come. Human technology may change according to the upscaled knowledge of humankind, but the First Technology of Light will never change, and it will continue shining as the Last Technology of Light in the everlasting Kingdom of Light of our sovereign Lord because the Almighty God of Great Technology of Light never changes!

No one on earth could create light from the pillar of cloud for Israelites during their 40 years in desert except the God of Great Technology of Light (Exod.13:21-22; Neh. 9:19 NRSV). In the Old Testament time, Isaiah prophesized that in the future Zion City there would not be any sun or moon needed, because the Lord will be the Light of Zion (Isa. 60:19 NRSV). In New Testament times, John saw a vision of the New Jerusalem in Heaven where the Lord will be the Light of that Heavenly City (Rev. 22:5 NRSV). Therefore, from the ancient time to the future time, the God of the First and the Last Technology of Light is the same. This is the Alpha and Omega God worshipped by Christians all over the world. *The Discover God* describes God's character:

> God never changes. In fact, it is impossible for God to change. The influence that causes change in your life have no effect on God. He will never be stronger or weaker. His knowledge and wisdom will not

increase or diminish. God does not compromise or change His values. And God does not have mood swings. Life and its uncertainties may shake you, but God—the Rock of Ages—does not move.[24]

Human technology may reach for the sky as ongoing AI technology rapidly advances in our time, but if there is no light in this world, this AI technology will be seen as just dead AI, because it will sink deep below the surface of darkness. Technology becomes useless without light. That First Technology of Light is the life of all technology, and it is the main source for any technology's life, so that obviously, it is the energy source of any future AI technology as well. If that First Technology of Light were shut down from the universe, the whole cosmos would go back to the Dark Age that existed before God's Creation.

Intelligent human technology and the civilized human world will always be under an everlasting umbrella of God's First Technology of Light. The Last Technology of Light will be shining in eternity after the all-earthy technologies are destroyed. Thus, God is always in control of both humanity and human technology through the ages, no matter whether people believe it or not. Poythress believes that "the better one knows God, the better one may predict how he governs the world."[25]

---

[24] DiscoverGod.com, "God Never Changes," accessed December 21, 2019, http://discovergod.com/character13.html.

[25] Vern S. Poythress, *Redeeming Science: A God-Center Approach* (Wheaton, IL: Crossway Books, 2006), 177.

The Growing of Humanoid-AI Robots

In this AI technology, many people wonder whether humanoid-AI robots may join leadership roles with other humans in factories or get into some leading positions in human society. The majority of respondents (88.1 %) to the *Human-AI Culture* survey do not want humanoid-AI robots to become their supervisors, counselors, or church leaders. Some respondents told me that they would not want to lose their jobs to AI robots while others shared that they could not trust heartless non-human leadership, because smart people really know the answer for the question *Are "These" Us?*

Daniel interpreted a last earthy kingdom, which will be one of mixed iron and clay feet. Most scholars in Daniel's time and people living after Daniel's time until the pre-AI technology of our time could not understand the metaphor as Daniel interpreted it (Dan. 2:41- 43 NRSV). No one could imagine that the mystery of mixed iron-clay feet might happen in our present time, the mixture between humanoid-AI robots and human beings—a metaphor of different seeds of two different source of beings, bio-technology beings and human beings. The singularity is near as Kurzweil claims.[26]

---

[26] Ray Kurzweil, *The Singularity Is Near* (New York, NY: Penguin Books, 2006), 9. The singularity will represent the culmination of the merger of our biological thinking and existence with our technology, resulting in a world that is still human but that transcends our biological roots. There will be no distinction, post-Singularity, between human and machine or between physical and virtual reality. If you wonder what will remain unequivocally human in such a world, it's

If humanoid-AI robots will be created to mimic human beings both in human-like embodiments and with human's intelligent brains, then Daniel's prophesy of the mixed seeds of iron and clay would become true. If AI robots are mass produced, there could be a kingdom on earth that is mixed between human-like machines and human beings, like the metaphor of mixed iron-clay feet in Daniel's interpretation.

According to Alex Lightman, "by 2025, more than 1.5 million robots will be operating on the planet, and we'll be seeing that exponential growth curve exhibited with that number doubling every year. By the early 2030s, robots are likely to outnumber humans."[27] When it was asked whether humanoid-AI would surpass human intelligence and dominate human beings in the near future: 55.2 percent of respondents to the *Human-AI Culture* survey disagreed that humanoid-AI robots will surpass human intelligence and take control over humanity, but the other half worried that it might happen soon in the future. However, if God has a way to control human population throughout human history, God will have the way to resolve a humanoid-AI population in the future.

In reality, humanoid-AI robots are not going to control humankind, but their creators might try to take control of the future of humanity. These creators are those who work for BAT and G-MAFIA. Amy Webb named them

---

simply this quality: ours is the species that inherently seeks to extend its physical and mental reach beyond current limitations.

[27] Brett King, *Augmented Life in the Smart Lane* (Tarrytown, NY: Marshall Cavendish, 2016), 123.

the Big Nine.[28] The BAT represents China's tech companies (Baidu, Alibaba and Tencent), and the G-MAFIA stands for the American tech giants (Google, Microsoft, Amazon, Facebook, IBM, and Apple). Russian president Vladimir Putin also claims: "Artificial intelligence is the future, not only for Russia, but for all humankind. It comes with colossal opportunities, but also threats that are difficult to predict. Whoever becomes the leader in this sphere will become the ruler of the world."[29]

Recently, someone tried to create an AI God and established "the Way of the Future" as the new way of religion to convince people to worship an AI god. This new religion may end up writing its own AI bible.[30]

---

[28] Amy Webb, *The Big Nine*, 96. The Big Nine-China's BAT (Baidu, Alibaba, and Tencent) and America's G-MAFIA (Google, Microsoft, Amazon, Facebook, IBM, and Apple)—are developing the tools and built the environment that will power the future of artificial intelligence.

[29] RT Question More, "'Whoever Leads in AI Will Rule the World': Putin to Russian Children on Knowledge Day," September 1, 2017, https://www.rt.com/news/401731-ai-rule-world-putin/.

[30] John Brandon, "An AI God Will Emerge by 2024 and Write Its Own Bible. Will You Worship It?," October 2, 2017, https://venturebeat.com/2017/10/02/an-ai-god-will-emerge-by-2042-and-write-its-own-bible-will-you-worship-it/. Recently, reports surfaced that a controversy plagued engineer who once worked at Uber has started a new religion. Anthony Lewandowsky filed paperwork for a nonprofit religious organization called The Way of the Future. Its mission: "To develop and promote the realization of a Godhead based on artificial intelligence and through understanding and worship of the Godhead contributed to the betterment of society.". . . An AI that is all-powerful in the next 25-50 years could decide to write a similar AI bible for humans to follow, one that matches its own collective intelligence.

Nevertheless, God is always in control of both human technology and human history. Isaiah proclaimed God's sovereignty over humanity, that incomprehensive mystery that no one could understand: "For my thoughts are not your thoughts, nor are your ways my ways, says the LORD. For as the heavens are higher than the earth, so are my ways higher than your ways and my thoughts than your thoughts" (Isa. 55:8-9 NRSV).

CONCLUSION

Facing the rapid change of science, technology, and cultural movement in human society, our young Christian generation is being swept away by the billowing flow of the era of artificial intelligence. There is a time in the advanced AI technological age, in which human beings may not ask ourselves the question 'Are *"These"* Us?,' but instead humorously ask each other 'Are we *"These"*?' This may happen at the point when humanoid-AI robots are overflowing as new habitants in our human world. Preparing us for that future mixed Human-AI culture, Kate Ott has asked the following question, appealing to Christians' rethinking: "what does Christianity have to offer to a digital world? Living as a Christian in a digital society calls us to rethinking faith values and practices."[31]

As a Christian, I believe that there will be huge changes in our digital society in the next couple of decades. Humans have dreamed to have something created in our

---

[31] Kate Ott, *Christian Ethics for a Digital Society* (New York: Rowman & Littlefield, 2019), 3.

image to test the limits of our human knowledge and wisdom and to have something to fill up the gaps of loneliness and brokenness in human hearts.

Christianity never rejects the great scientific achievements, but never agrees that science is "another God." Christians also believe that science will not be able to replace the presence of God and the Lord's sovereignty in the whole universe, not even as human wisdom reaches for the clouds. Christian ethical, redemptive, and theological practices are aimed to save full human beings regardless of who, what, or how they are, since God's salvation is for all humankind, who carry the image of God and a soul in a human flesh-blood embodiment.

The metaphor of the mixed iron-clay feet in Daniel's prophecy could happen in the age of AI technology in which human beings blended with humanoid-AI machines. Semiotically, if our life, the temple of God, is built as the City of Light, we need to shine our light and reach out to our human community to save as many people as we can before the day of rapture when humans still have a chance to know Jesus, the Light of Life, and the Savior of humankind. Communicating our dynamic Christian faith in a potentially mixed Human-AI culture is to offer openness and loving kindness to those fully human beings, who are lonely and broken in their relationship with the Creator and with other human beings in this chaotic AI technology age. According to Ron Clark, our God is the *God of Second Chances*; thus, "however, when humans choose the worst, or choose not to act, God has another option. Because God knows all things, sees the future and leaves destiny open, God is aware of multiple options."[32] Though people can reject or accept Jesus' Gospel through our shining faith, Twesigye urges us: "Positive and dynamic religious faith is universally an essential perquisite for religion, love and an open satisfying social life. Faith is the courage to be human and the power for living a finite human life in a capricious world."[33] Only our dynamic faith will encourage humans to pursue opportunities to be healed, to be recovered, to be loved, and to be saved by the grace of God. This also helps Christians to fulfill our mission on earth reaching out to the end of the world with the dynamic love from Jesus' Gospel to prepare humankind for the eternal life in the Kingdom of Heaven.

Christians should not live-in fear of what is going to happen to the world of humanity in the age of AI technology and the chaotic of this lost world since our God is the Alpha and the Omega God, who is always in control. Our Christian belief is based on the Creator of the First Technology of Light that began God's Creation in the beginning and continues light up our faith into eternity in the Kingdom of Light to come. The darker the midnight of the end time would be, the closer the dawn of our faith to transform us into eternity would come.

If the God of the Old Testament said: "Do not fear, for I am with you, do not be afraid, for I am your God; I will

---

[32] Ron Clark, The God of Second Chances: Finding Hope through the Prophets of Exile (Eugene, OR: Wipf and Stock, 2012), 103.

[33] Emmanuel K. Twesigye, *Religion and Ethics for a New Age: Evolutionist Approach* (Lanham, MD: University Press of America, 2001), 35.

strengthen you, I will help you, I will uphold you with my victorious right hand (Isa. 41:10 NRSV), the God of the New Testament says: "because I live, you also will live (John 14:19 NRSV). As Christians, we have hope, faith, and salvation await us ahead in the end time because "Jesus Christ is the same yesterday and today and forever" (Heb. 13:8 NRSV). This is our dynamic Christian faith that never dies, it becomes our Christian pride, and it is always the greatest guide in our lives, to shine the gracious love and the glory of Jesus Christ on earth as in Heaven.

CHAPTER 6:
CONCLUSION

Human dreams are beautiful, and human imagination often opens a new horizon of creativity in which it lifts up humankind beyond the reach of other creatures and significantly changes the fate of humanity in the whole cosmos. From ancient times to the present time, because of human dreams, civilization ceaselessly increases with the birth of new technology through different ages. No dreamed stories from other creatures on our planet would be told and retold on earth, except those of humankind, which has led the wings of their dreams across the ocean, reached far away continents, soared on clouds, and echoed from endless galaxies to convey their stories from one generation to the next.

Human dreams are of various types, from unreal to real, from nonsense to valuable, from fake to true. That is why many valuable human dreams are regarded as illusions and are often forgotten over time. However, human dreams were important for people in ancient times. Sigmund Freud said: "The ancients distinguished between the true and valuable dreams which were sent to the dreamer as warnings, or to foretell future events, and the vain, fraudulent, and empty dreams whose object was to misguide him or lead him to destruction."[34] Thus, kings and queens often have magicians, enchanters, or sorcerers around them to help

---

[34] Sigmund Freud, *The Major Work of Sigmund Freud* (New York, NY: William Benton, 1939), 138.

unveil the mysteries of their dreams.

In Babylonian times, when the Jews were captives in the Babylonian kingdom, God revealed to a tyrant, Nebuchadnezzar, the mystery of the future through his dream, to let him know that there is a Living God who controls not only the fortune of his own life but also the fate of humankind. That awaking dream had gone from his memory like the night had faded away before the dawn light, and it troubled him like a threat from a ghost of his enemy. A dream could become a guardian angel or a night thief to bless or to steal the lives of kings and their dynasties. Thus, the mystery of Nebuchadnezzar's dream almost cost the lives of all the magicians and enchanters in his kingdom, if Daniel, a Judahite noble slave, was not to be found in Nebuchadnezzar's palace among the courtiers of the king. Nebuchadnezzar held power in his hand, but he could not hold the future. Only God could hold the future and showed Nebuchadnezzar that "Not by might, nor by power, but by my spirit, says the LORD of hosts" (Zech. 4:6 NRSV). Daniel was a messenger from God sent to Nebuchadnezzar to alert him that all earthly kings fall under God's control. Only God knows the right timing for the rise and fall of all kingdoms on earth, as God revealed to Nebuchadnezzar through his dream of a humanoid metallic image.

On the one hand, Nebuchadnezzar's dream revealed the changing of human political power throughout human history. On the other hand, Nebuchadnezzar's dream was not a myth but a mirror that reflects how humanity uses God's bestowed ruling power to act upon humankind and other creatures in the universe through human technology.

Nebuchadnezzar's dream of a humanoid metallic statue interpreted by Daniel told the king not only of the fate of humanity but also of the various technologies to be developed through the different stages of human civilization.

If the metallic humanoid statue decreased from the most to the least value metal, from Gold head to Silver chest and arms, to Bronze belly and thigh, to Iron legs, to mixed iron-clay feet—until the stone from heaven struck down the whole statue, if the statue carries a message of human political power systems decaying throughout human history and ending in God's assigned time, then why aren't the feet of the statue in Nebuchadnezzar's dream a mixture of two metals such as iron-gold, iron- silver, or iron-bronze? Why are they instead a mixture between two materials with significant different attributes—iron and clay?

Naturally, the mixture of two metals together can have less value, they may stick well together, form a stronger material, and increase its strength and hardness, such as the alloy of gold and silver will form white gold, and the alloy of gold and copper will become red gold,[35] and the alloy of

---

[35] Wikipedia.com, "Alloy," accessed November 30, 2019, https://en.wikipedia.org/wiki/Alloy. An alloy is a combination of metals or a combination of one or more metals with non-metallic elements. For example, combining the metallic elements gold and copper produces red gold, gold and silver becomes white gold, and silver combined with copper produces sterling silver. Elemental iron, combined with non-metallic carbon or silicon, produces alloys called steel or silicon steel. The resulting mixture forms a substance with properties that often differ from those of the pure metals, such as increased strength or hardness.

gold and iron will form a blue gold.[36] The new form of these two-metallic alloys would last permanently, and it would not be a good metaphor for the end time of human history. Thus, God showed the mixed iron-clay feet metaphor to emphasize that the human world is temporary and will be ended in its due time.

The metaphor of the mixed iron-clay feet, a representation of the last earthly kingdom before the end of the human world, could have different interpretations. One of the most applicable interpretations of that iron-clay feet metaphor is the semiotic view of the mixed humanoid-AI and human beings in the AI technology age, in which humanoid-AI robots and humanity represent the iron and the clay portion of the feet respectively.

Why was this mixed iron-clay feet not considered in prior technological ages? During the agricultural revolution that happened in the 18th century, technology has helped farmers cut down their time on the field, because they could produce more food with fewer labors. Farming equipment such as tractors, combines, and plows are bigger and work faster than buffaloes and horses, but they are still mechanical machines, like cars, trucks, etc.[37]

---

[36] Anne Marie Helmenstine, "Composition of Gold Alloys in Colored Gold Jewery," updated January 27, 2019, https://www.thoughtco.com/composition-of-gold-alloys-608016.

[37] AnimalSmart.org, "Comparing Agriculture of the Past with Today," accessed December 10, 2019, https://animalsmart.org/animals-and-the-environment/comparing-agriculture-of-the-past-with-today. Farmers use technology to make advances in producing more food for a growing world. Through the use of technology, each farmer is able to

During the industrial revolution in the second half of the 18th century—the first industrial revolution—to the late 19th century and early 20th century, "that transformed largely rural, agrarian societies in Europe and America into industrialized, urban ones,"[38] significant changes happened in human society through new technology innovations. Those remarkable innovations during the Industrial revolution were the Weaving engine invented by James Hargreaves in 1764, the Newcomen steam engine by Thomas Newcomen in 1712, the Watt steam engine by a Scottish engineer James Watt in 1776, the locomotives, the 'Pen-y-deren' by Richard Trevithick in 1812, and the Rocket by George and Robert Stephenson in 1837. The industrial revolution also saw inventions, such as the telegraph for communications by Sir William Fothergill Cooke and Charles Wheatstone in 1837 and the Morse Code by an American Samuel Morse, Dynamite by a Swedish Chemist Alfred Nobel in 1860s, the photograph by a French

---

feed 155 people today, compared to 1940, when one farmer could feed only 19 people. Farmers use technologies such as motorized equipment, modified housing for animals and biotechnology, which allow for improvement in agriculture. Better technology has allowed farmers to feed more people and requires fewer people to work on farms to feed their families. Changes in equipment have made a large impact on the way farmers are able to farm and grow food. In the past, farmers would have to do field work by hand or with horse-drawn equipment. . . Today, most farmers use tractors and other motorized equipments to help with field work. Tractors, combines, plows, etc. are much larger and move much faster than horses, so farmers are able to produce more food in a shorter amount of time.

[38] History.com, "Industrial Revolution," updated September 9, 2019, https://www.history.com/topics/industrial-revolution/industrial-revolution.

inventor Joseph Nicéphore Niépce in 1826, the typewriter by an American inventor William Burt in 1829, the electric generator Faraday Disk by Michael Faraday in 1831, and the modern factory by Richard Arkwright in 1771.[39]

However, the industrial revolution brought forth machines that helped to improve human life and technology, that brought civilization to the human world. Humans and machines cooperated to offer tremendous benefits to humanity. Nowadays, scientists and technology developers have tried to create a new biotechnological non-human seed similar to the human seed, not only to work but to live alongside humans, to love and to be loved as a loving partner of human beings. If AI technology advances in the near future, it would not only create a huge amount of AI robots to replace the human workforce but could also give birth to a new humanoid-AI community that will mix with real human communities to form a new mixed Human-AI culture.

If human history proved the golden Babylonian kingdom had failed, that the Silver chest and arms of the Mede-Persian kingdom failed, then that the bronze belly and thigh of Greece failed, then that the iron legs of the Roman Empire failed, then human history will go through the mixed iron-clay kingdom before the stone from heaven destroys all earthly kingdoms in the end time. This mixed iron-clay kingdom has been understood to be the ongoing kingdom

---

[39] Tristan Hughes, "10 Key Inventors of the Industrial Revolution," November 27, 2018, https://www.historyhit.com/key-inventions-of-the-industrial-revolution/.

after the reign of the Roman Empire until the end time. Perhaps it will be the mixture between human and the AI technology of our time.

Semiotically, humanoid-AI robots and human beings would be a perfect match to the mixed iron-clay feet—the mixture between biotechnological and the biological fully human embodiments in the feet of Human-AI culture. That metaphor could be interpreted differently, but the biological seed of full humanness combining with the seeds of biotechnology AI would fit in well with Daniel's interpretation of seeds between two types of humans that can marry each other but not cling together (Dan. 2:43 NRSV).

Christianity may have some issues in adopting this semiotic interpretation of Daniel's mixed iron-clay feet as a proper application of a potentially mixed human-AI culture in the age of AI technology. However, no other technological age throughout human history provoked a significant thought of creating humanoid-AI machines to mimic both human beings' physique and consciousness like what is happening in the AI technology of our time. Since the Turing test gave birth to the new trait of thinking machines, scientists and technological innovators have tried hard to create humanoid-AI machines not only doing 'three Ds," job categories—the dull, dirty, or dangerous jobs—that cost humans' sweat, tears, and blood; but also do the "fourth D" job, the Deep Learning skill of the human brain. Furthermore, scientists moved beyond the limits of preserving the precious full humanness of humankind by creating human-AI machines with sensing embodiments and consciousness to the levels of human intelligence to communicate and to have loving relationship with humans, even to make decisions for human beings. Perhaps, this was done in order to be able to fill the gaps of human loneliness and brokenness in the relationship with both the Creator and with other human beings.

However, to create humanoid-AI machines to mimic the human brain, to acquire consciousness and soul, to surpass human intelligence levels, to become humans' soulmates, or to marry human beings, that would be considered a risky ethical approach, because those attributes are applied only to humanity, fully-human creatures who are created in the image of God. Thus, losing our image of God to humanoid-AI robots is losing our most valuable identity of full humanness, our representative role of God's bestowed ruling power over other creatures, and at some point in the future we will lose our precious human rights to non-human machines. Potentially, at that time we may ask ourselves the question 'Are We becoming *"These"?'* instead of 'Are *"These"* Us?'

If this would happen as the AI technology advances soon, a mixed Human-AI culture would come into existence in the human world, and Daniel's prophecy of the mixed iron-clay metaphor would come true to warn us that the end time of humanity is near. What would be the fate of humankind in the new kingdom of humanoid-AI robots mixing with human beings, iron beings and clay beings, the stronger Frubber-electric physical and digital brain beings, and the weaker flesh-blood embodiment and biological brain beings.

Are *"These"* Us?

Are "*These*" Us? would be the first question that any human being could ask when we see a humanoid-AI robot living in our neighborhood. For Christians, we curiously wonder whether a humanoid-AI carries the image of God, has a soul, or receives God's salvation. Most Christians believe that only human beings carry the image of God, have souls, and receive God's salvation regardless of who, what, and how people are, because all humans are all equal in God's eyes at any technology age, in any level of human civilization. These gracious privileges will never be taken away from humankind. However, *These*, the heartless and soulless sophisticated humanoid-AI machines would not be considered as bearing the same full humanness as humans; thus *These* could not inherit the same opportunity of salvation as humanity does.

What if humanoid-AI robots inherit all human intelligence programmed in their digital brain in their tireless embodiment? What if *These* would replace the human workforce, take away our jobs? This worry is a controversy in our time, and it will be answered by time just as we have seen it repeatedly answered by our forefathers throughout the agricultural and industrial revolutions in previous centuries. A Vietnamese proverb says: "God creates elephants, God provides grass." This promotes an idea of our Creator as a great provider. Since the elephant could eat all the grass or even trample the grass under their feet, the grass would not all die since the root of the grass is under ground. New grass will grow on earth. Similarly, if humanoid AI robots take over some of our jobs, new types of jobs, better jobs will grow out of the old ones for humanity in the Human-AI society. Jesus said:

> Therefore, do not worry, saying, 'What will we eat?' or 'What will we drink?' or 'What will we wear?' For it is the Gentiles who strive for all these things; and indeed, your heavenly Father knows that you need all these things. But strive first for the kingdom of God and his righteousness, and all these things will be given to you as well. "So do not worry about tomorrow, for tomorrow will bring worries of its own. Today's trouble is enough for today (Matt. 6:31-34 NRSV).

What if, at some point in the future, *These* will surpass human intelligence and dominate humankind and force us to do something against our will, how should we respond to that? In reality, humanoid AI will never surpass human intelligence. We create them, they do not create us. Even though some individuals among us may have less IQ than a humanoid-AI machine, the creators of humanoid-AI robots are human beings among us. We are intelligent people, and we can handle the critical issues that a humanoid-AI community troubles us with, unless some of those intelligent people turn into dictators to take control of the future of humanity. Thus, humanoid-AI robots may not harm us or force us to do those things, but their creators, who programmed *These* with fixed algorithms may do so. *These* are simply digital machines that carry digital brains in humanoid-AI bodies.

According to Amy Webb, the Big Nine or the BAT and G-MAFIA—Chinese tech companies (Baidu, Alibaba and Tencent), and American tech giants (Google, Microsoft, Amazon, Facebook, IBM, and Apple)—are the creators of the AI technology of our time. They may try to take control of the human world through AI technology, the most powerful digital life on earth. However, Jesus said: "Do not fear those who kill the body but cannot kill the soul; rather fear him who can destroy both soul and body in hell" (Matt. 10:28 NRSV), "and remember, I am with you always, to the end of the age" (Matt. 28:20 NRSV).

Some people may wonder if humanoid-AI robots will be seen in Heaven. If there are, we will have those humanoid robots in Heaven as our servants as other angels. Those humanoid-AI robots in Heaven were not created by human hands from this lost world since *These,* the earthly humanoid AI robots with their sophisticated Frubber smooth skin and their AI-Neutral brains, would never survive through the Fire of the Holy Spirit.

In the beginning, the Spirit of God was hovering over the surface of the darkness to calm down the chaos in the cosmos, to remove the fearful messes, and to bring out the gratefulness into God's Creation. Then, the First Technology of Light birthed out and brought the new light, new hope, and new life to the new Creation world. Similarly, in our present time, the Holy Spirit of God will work throughout the whole world to calm down all chaos in this lost world: to remove fearfulness, and to bring faithfulness in this new age of AI technology full of chaos and sorrow. The First Technology of Light is still shining new light, new hope, and new life throughout Creation to Eternity.

Ron Clark, a minister who has tried to preserve the image of God among those who are abused, neglected, and exploited, and living on the dirty sidewalks of life, has offered a motif of Christian life in this sinful world: "If we model the reality of peace, justice, hope, love, and compassion, then the kingdom of God has again come upon us. It is here, but needs our voice to spread."[40]

Leonard Sweet promotes some good thoughts on changing the world in his *Preach the Story:* "Do you really think that having the right theology, or the right politics, or the right economics, or the right stuff, will bring lasting change to our world? Only the right heart, a metanoia and a metamorphosis, will bring lasting change. Church, rise up and tell what only you can tell."[41]

Thus, Christians should communicate our faith with openness and loving kindness to those who are hurt, lonely, or broken in the potentially mixed Human-AI culture, where humans are wandering and lost in the dark jungle of life and dead valley of civilized technology. No matter how Satan would repeatedly try to trap humankind under the Silicon Valley of Death and the Dark Age of technology, the First Technology of Light of our Alpha and Omega God will

---

[40] Ron Clark, "*Our Thoughts and Experiences on Prostitudes and Trafficking*," Facebook, September 6, 2011, https://www.facebook.com/notes/ron-clark/our-thoughts-and-experiences-on-prostitution-and-trafficking/10150312432398303/.

[41] Leonard Sweet, "Preach the Story," Facebook, February 27, 2020, https://www.facebook.com/PreachtheStory/posts/3342547759094724?__tn__=-R.

never die out. God will still generate a beautiful rainbow of hope to proclaim God's gracious love and merciful redemption through the Rock of All Ages, Jesus Christ—the Way, the Truth, and the Life—for all humankind (John 14:6 NRSV).

APPENDIX A:

HUMAN-AI CULTURE SURVEY [42]

1a. When AI is advancing in the near future: Do you think that humanoid AI robots bring more benefits than dangers to the human world?
270 responses

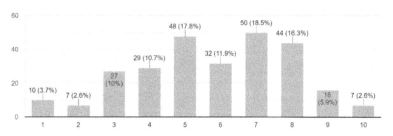

1b. Do you think humanoid AI robots will replace human workforce and take away people's jobs?
270 responses

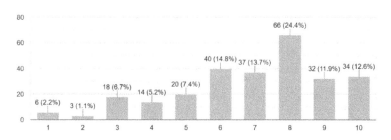

[42] Hoa Huu Nguyen, "Human-AI Culture," accessed February 12, 2019, https://docs.google.com/forms/d/1CF9jN1vB5ZaOUgoxM1uTh34wwA rDhnjszhEnmuKiJgw/edit#responses.

2. Do you feel more secure if you live among humanoid AI robots in the near future?

270 responses

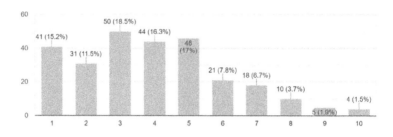

3. Do you feel that an Amazon Alexa or a Google Smart Speaker might invade your privacy if you own one?

271 responses

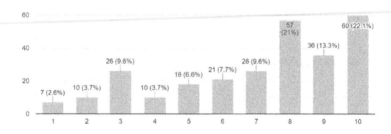

4. If humanoid AI robots surpass human intelligence, will AI robots dominate human beings in the near future?

270 responses

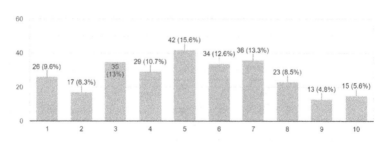

5. As AI technology advances in the near future, and humanoid AI robots can be "perfectly" created, will they ...the Image of God" as human beings do?
271 responses

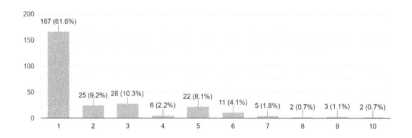

6a. If humanoid AI robots becomes more conscious and self-aware: Do you think that a humanoid AI robot will have a soul?
270 responses

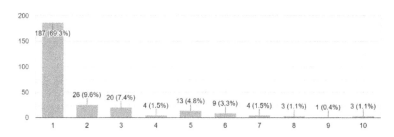

6b. Can a humanoid AI robot receive God's salvation?
268 responses

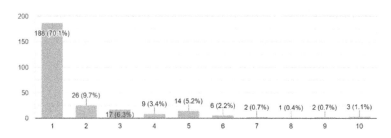

7. If humans consider to have a robot sex partner and to marry a humanoid AI robot in the near future, do you agr...dding ceremony in your future church?

267 responses

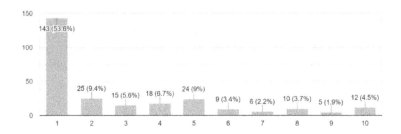

8. Will you agree to have a chip inserted in your body (hands, forehead, etc.) to be able to do your daily business or...pted as a member of a certain society?

267 responses

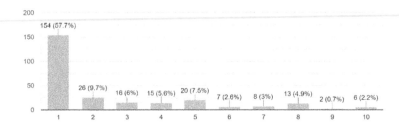

9. Will you be comfortable to have a humanoid AI robot as your supervisor, counselor, or church leader?

269 responses

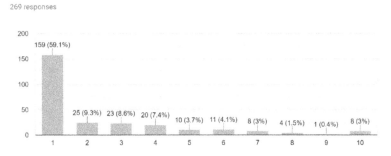

10. An ex-Google engineer is forming a first church of AI and trying to create an "AI God" to rule over humans...e "666" Beast in Revelation 13:15-18?

269 responses

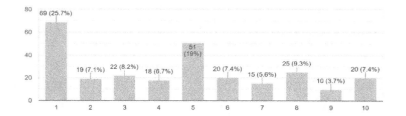

BIBLIOGRAPHY

Ahire, Jayesh Bapu. *Artificial Neural Networks: The Brian Behind AI.* England: AI Research, 2018.

Ancient Origins. "Throwing Virgins into the Sea and Other Ways to Appease the Gods: The Ancient Reasons behind Virgin Sacrifice." October 9, 2017. https://www.ancient-origins.net/history/ throwing-virgins-sea-and-other-ways-appease-gods-ancient-reasons-behind-virgin-sacrifice-021653.

AnimalSmart.org. "Comparing Agriculture of the Past with Today." Accessed December 10, 2019. https://animalsmart.org/animals-and-the-environment/comparing-agriculture-of-the-past-with-today.

Arner, Lynn. "History Lesson from the End of Time: Gower and the English Rising of 1381." *Clio* 31, no. 3 (2002): 237-255. ProQuest.

Austin, Jon. "MARK OF THE BEAST: Secret Plan to 'Implant Us All with ID Chips by 2017'." August 25, 2016. https://www.express.co.uk/news/weird/703856/MARK-OF-THE-BEAST-Secret-plan-to-implant-us-all-with-ID-chips-by-2017.

Bellis, Marry. "Who Pioneered Robotics?" ThoughtCo. Updated February 03, 2019. https://www.thoughtco.com/timeline-of-robots-1992363.

BibleHub. "Barnes' Notes on the Bible: Revelation 22:13." Accessed December 21, 2019. https://biblehub.com/commentaries/revelation/22-13.htm.

_____. 'Benson Commentary: Daniel 2:40-43." Accessed October 15, 2019. https://biblehub.com/commentaries/benson/daniel/2.htm.

_____. "Daniel 2: Gill's Exposition." Accessed July 8, 2019. https://biblehub.com/commentaries/gill/daniel/2.html.

_____. "Daniel 2: Benson's Commentary." Accessed July 8, 2019. https://biblehub.com/commentaries/benson/daniel/2.htm.

_____. "Matthew Henry's Concise Commentary: Daniel 2:31." Accessed October 15, 2019. https://biblehub.com/commentaries/mhc/daniel/2.htm.

_____. "Matthew Henry's Concise Commentary: Daniel 2:33." Accessed October 15, 2019. https://biblehub.com/commentaries/daniel/2-33.htm.

Biography Online. "Major Periods in Human History." Accessed September 30, 2019. https://www.biographyonline.net/ different-periods-in-history/.

Bloomfield, Arthur E. *The End of the Days*. Minneapolis, MN: Bethany Fellowship, 1961.

Brandon, John. "An AI God Will Emerge by 2024 and Writes Its Own Bible. Will You Worship It?" October 2, 2017. https://venturebeat.com/2017/10/02/an-ai-god-will-emerge-by-2042-and-write-its-own-bible-will-you-worship-it/.

Brook, John Hedley. *Science and Religion: Some Historical Perspectives*. New York, NY: Cambridge University Press, 2014.

Brundage, Matt. "The Meaning of Thomas Jefferson's Phrase 'All Men Are Created Equal.'" Accessed October 25, 2019. https://www.mattbrundage.com/ publications/jefferson-equality/.

Carraway, Bryan. "A Theological Look at Spiritual Dreams." Accessed February 12, 2020, https://www1.cbn.com/theological-look-spiritual-dreams.

Ciaccia, Chris. "Robots Will Be 100 Times Smarter than Humans in 30 Years, Tech Expert Says," October 27, 2017, https://www.foxnews.com/tech/robots-will-be-100-times-smarter-than-huamn-in-30-years-tech-exec-says.

Clark, Kelly James. *Religion and Sciences of Origins: History and Contemporary Discussions.* New York, NY: Palgrave Macmillan, 2014.

Clark, Ron. "Our Thoughts and Experiences on Prostitutes and Trafficking." Facebook. September 6, 2011. https://www.facebook.com/notes/ron-clark/our-thoughts-and-experiences-on-prostitution-and-trafficking/10150312432398303/.

_____. *The God of Second Chances: Finding Hope through the Prophets of Exile.* Eugene, OR: Wipf and Stock Publishers, 2012.

Clarke, Neil. ed. *More Human than Human: Stories of Androids, Robots, and Manufactured Humanity.* New York, NY: Night Shade Books, 2017.

Cohen, Eric. *In the Shadow of Progress: Being Human in the Age of Technology.* July 15, 2008. New York, NY: Encounter Books, 2008. https://ebookcentral-proquest-com.georgefox.idm.oclc.org/lib.

Collins, John J. Daniel: *A Commentary on the Book of Daniel.* Minneapolis, MN: Fortress Press, 1993.

David, Jeremiah. *Agents of Babylon: What the Prophet Daniel Tells Us about the End of Days.* Carol Stream, IL: Tyndale House, 2015.

DiscoverGod.com, "God Never Changes." Accessed December 21, 2019. http://discovergod.com/character13.html.

Dobson, Edward G. *Making the Right Choices.* Grand Rapids, MI: Baker Book House, 1994.

Downing, Crystal L. *Changing Signs of Truth: A Christian Introduction to the Semiotics of Communication.* Downers Grove, IL: InterVarsity Press, 2012.

End Time prophesy, "Kingdoms of Nebuchadnezzar's Image." Accessed October 25, 2019. http://www.end-times-prophecy. org/end-time-kingdom.html.

Enns, Peter. *The Evolution of Adam: What the Bible Does and Doesn't Say about Human Origins.* Grand Rapids, MI: Brazos Press, 2012.

Fox News. "Ray Kurzweil Predicts Computers Will Be as Smart as Humans in 12 Year." March 16, 2017. https://www.foxnews.com/tech/ray-kurzweil-predicts-computers-will-be-as-smart-as-humans-in-12-years.

Fox, Robin Lane. *Alexander the Great.* New York, NY: Penguin Books, 2004.

Frankish, Keith and William M. Ramsey. *The Cambridge Handbook of Artificial Intelligence. Cambridge,* UK: Cambridge University Press, 2014.

Fung, Justin. "Faith and Technology: Who Is in Control?" January 26, 2012. https://www.washingtonpost.com/local/faith-and-technology-who-is-in-control/2012/01/25/gIQArVpHTQ_ story.html.

Geraci, Robert M. *Apocalyptic AI: Vision of Heaven in Robotics, Artificial Intelligence, and Virtual Reality.* New York, NY: Oxford University Press, 2010.

Gershgorn, Dave. "Inside the Mechanical Brain of the World's First Robot Citizen." Quartz, November 12, 2017. https://qz.com/1121547/how-smart-is-the-first-robot- citizen/.

Grasso, Samantha. "Human-Robot Marriage Could Be Legal by 2050, Experts Say," November 26, 2016. https://www.dailydot.com/debug/sex-robot-human-marriage-legal-2050/.

Greenblatt, Stephen. *The Rise and Fall of Adam and Eve.* New York: W.W. Norton, 2017.

Greene, Oliver B. *Daniel: Verse by Verse Study.* Greenville, SC: Gospel House, 1964.

Gurney, Robert. *God in Control.* Worthing West Sussex, England: H.E Walter, 1980.

Haarsma, Debora B. and Loren Haarsma. *Origins: Christian Perspectives on Creation, Evolution, and Intelligent Design.* Grand Rapids, MI: Faith Alive Christian Resources, 2011.

Hansen Robotic. "Creating Value with Human-Like Robots." Accessed November 30, 2019. https://www.hansonrobotics.com/hanson-robots/.

_____. "Why Human-Like Robots?" Accessed October 25, 2019. https://www.hansonrobotics.com/.

Harari, Yuval Noah. *Homo Deus: A Brief History of Humankind.* New York, NY: HarperCollins, 2017.

Harris, Michael C. *Artificial Intelligence.* New York, NY: Marshall Cavendish Benchmark, 2011.

HearingSol. "The Five Senses of the Human Body: Facts, Figure, and Functionality." Accessed November 20, 2019. https://www.hearingsol.com/articles/facts-five-sense-organs-of-human-body/.

Helmenstine, Anne Marie. "Composition of Gold Alloys in Colored Jewelry." Updated January 27, 2019. https://www.thoughtco.com/composition-of-gold-alloys-608016.

Herzfeld, Noreen, Nancy Murphy, and Christopher C. Knight, eds. *Human Identity at the Intersection of Science, Technology and Religion.* Burlington, VT: Ashgate, 2010.

_____. "Industrial Revolution." Updated September 9, 2019." https://www.history.com/topics/industrial-revolution/industrial-revolution.

Hughes, Tristan. "10 Key Inventors of the Industrial Revolution." November 27, 2018. https://www.historyhit.com/key-inventions-of-the-industrial-revolution.

Jersild, Paul. *Christian Faith in Our Time: Rethinking the Church's Theology.* Eugene, OR: Wipf and Stock, 2016. ProQuest Ebook Central.

Jongko, Paul. "Ten Ancient Cultures That Practiced Ritual Human Sacrifice." Posted July 29, 2014. https://www.toptenz.net/10-ancient-cultures-practiced-ritual-human-sacrifice.php.

King, Brett. *Augmented Life in the Smart Lane.* Tarrytown, NY: Marshall Cavendish, 2016.

King, Geoffrey R. *Daniel: A Detailed Explanation of the Book.* Grand Rapids, MI: Wm. B. Eerdmans, 1966.

King, Philip J. and Loren E. Stager. *Life in Biblical Israel.* Louisville, KY: Westminster John Knox Press, 2001.

Kugel, James L. *How to Read the Bible: A Guide to Scripture, Then and Now.* New York, NY: Free Press, 2017.

Kurzweil, Ray. *The Singularity Is Near.* New York, NY: Penguin Books, 2006.

Lanier, Jaron. *You Are Not A Gadget: A Manifesto*. New York, NY: Random House, 2011.

Lee, Kai-Fu. "Tech Companies Should Stop Pretending AI Won't Destroy Jobs." *MIT Technology Review* 121, no. 2 (March 2018): 9. EBSCOhost.

Leston, Stephen. *The Bible in World History: How History and Scripture Intersect.* Uhrichsville, OH: Barbour Books House, 2011.

Levi, David. *Robot Unlimited: Life in a Virtual Age.* Wellesley, MA: A K Peters, 2006.

Lexico.com. "Lexico Dictionary Powered by Oxford." Accessed December 10, 2018. https://www.lexico.com/en/definition/artificial-Intelligence.

Lin, Patrick, Keith Abney, and George A. Berkey, ed. *Robot Ethics: The Ethical and Social Implication of Robotics*. Cambridge, Mass: MIT Press, 2012.

Lumen, Boundless Biology. "Components of Blood." Accessed November 20, 2019. https://courses.lumenlearning.com/boundless-biology/chapter/components-of-the-blood/.

Makehow.com. "Industrial Robots." Accessed July 29, 2019. http://www.madehow.com/Volume-2/Industrial-Robot.html#ixzz5vqwPrLPt.

Martin, Thomas R. *Ancient Greek: From prehistoric to Hellenistic Times*. New Haven: Yale University Press, 2013.

McDonald, Keza. "Being Human: How Realistic Do We Want Robots to Be?." June 27, 2018. https://www.theguardian.com/technology/2018/jun/27/being-human-realistic-robots-google-assistant-androids.

McGuire, Paul. "All Americans to Receive Microchip Soon." July 30, 2012. http://newswithviews.com/McGuire/paul136.htm.

McMillan, Wendy. *Amazed Clay*. Mustang, OK: Tate Publishing and Enterprises, 2010.

McMullan. "The World of God: How AI Is Defined in the Age of Secularism. January 18, 2018. https://medium.com/s/living-in-the-machine/the-word-of-god-how-ai-is-deified-in-the-age-of-secularism-5b24248f478e.

McNutt, Paula M. *The Forging of Israel: Iron Technology, Symbolism and Tradition in Ancient Society, the Social World of Biblical Antiquity*. Decatur, GA: Sheffield: Academic Press, 1990.

Metzger, Bruce M. and Michael D. Coogan, ed. *The Oxford Guide to People and Place of The Bible*. New York, NY: Oxford University Press, 2001.

Mills, Terence, Forbes Technology Council, "How Far Are We from Truly Human-Like AI? Accessed September 30, 2019. https://www.forbes.com/sites/forbestechcouncil/201 8/08/28/how-far-are-we-from-truly-human-like-ai/#16304feb31ac.

Morabito, Andrea. "Spouse-Swapping Reality Show 'Seven Year Switch' Ends with a Divorce," August 25, 2015. https://nypost.com/2015/08/25/spouse-swapping-reality-show-seven-year-switch-ends-with-a-divorce/.

Muhly, James D. "How Iron Technology Changed the Ancient World and Gave the Philistines a Military Edge." *Biblical Archaeology Review* 8, no. 6 (Nov-Dec 1982). https://www.baslibrary.org/biblical-archaeology-review/8/6/5.

Muller, John Paul and Luca Massaron. *Artificial Intelligence for Dummies*. Hoboken, NJ: John Willey and Son, 2018.

Nagler, Jorg. "American Study Journal: Abraham Lincoln' Attitudes on Slavery and Race." Accessed October 25, 2019. http://www.asjournal.org/53-2009/abraham-lincolns-attitudes-on-slavery-and-race/.

Nardo, Don. *World History Series: The Persian Empire*. San Diego, CA: Lucent Books, 1998.

National Post. "Thousands of Swedes Are Inserting Microchips into Themselves – Here's Why." June 25, 2018. https://nationalpost.com/news/world/thousands-of-swedes-are-inserting-microchips-into-themselves-heres-why.

Nelson, William B. *Daniel: Understanding the Bible Commentary Series.* Grand Rapids, MI: Baker Books, 2012.

Newsom, Carol A. *Daniel: The Old Testament Library.* Louisville, KY: Westminster John Knox Press, 2014.

Nguyen, Hoa Huu. "Human-AI Culture." Accessed November 20, 2019. https://docs.google.com/forms/d/1CF9jN1vB5ZaO UgoxM1uTh34wwArDhnjszhEnmuKiJgw/edit#responses.

Ott, Kate. *Christian Ethics for a Digital Society.* New York: Rowan & Littlefield, 2019.

Oxford Leaner's Dictionaries. Accessed September 20, 2019. https://www.oxfordlearners dictionaries.com/us/definition/ameican_enigliash/artificial_intelligence.

Pedersen, Daniel Pedersen and Christopher Lilley, eds. *Human Origin and the Image of God: Essay in Honor of J. Wentzel Van Huyssteen.* Grand Rapids, MI: William B Eerdmans, 2017. ProQuest Ebook Central.

Poythress, Vern S. *Redeeming Science: A God-Center Approach.* Wheaton, IL: Crossway Books, 2006.

Quantumrun.com, "What 2050 Will Look Like: Future Forecast." Accessed September 20, 2019. https://www.quantumrun.com/ future-timeline/2050#technology0.

Raymond, Robert. *Out of the Fiery Furnace: The Impact of Metals on the History of Mankind.* University Park, PA: Pennsylvania State University Press, 1986.

ResearchGate, "Sexrobotic: Acceptance and Options of use in Sex Therapy (Preprint)." February 2019. https://www.researchgate.net/publication/33142488 9_Sexrobotic_ Acceptance_and_options_of_use_in_sex_therapy_P reprint.

Revelation Timeline Decoded. "The Iron-Clay-Feet of Daniel 2." Accessed September 25, 2019. http://revelationtimelinedecoded.com/the-iron-clay-feet-of-daniel-2.

Reynoso, Rebecca. "The Complete History of Artificial Intelligence." Accessed April 12, 2019. https://learn.g2crowd.com/history-of-artificial-intelligence.

Rice University. "Nearly 70 Percent of Evangelical Do Not View Religion, Science as Being in Conflict." March 13, 2015. https://phys.org/news/2015-03-percent-evangelicals-view-religion-science.html.

RT Question More. "'Whoever Leads in AI Will Rule the World': Putin to Russian Children on Knowledge Day." September 1, 2017. https://www.rt.com/news/401731-ai-rule-world-putin.

Ryan, Kevin J. "Elon Musk (and 350 Experts) Predict exactly when Artificial Intelligence Will Overtake Human Intelligence." Published June 26, 2019. https://www.inc.com/kevin-j-ryan/elon-musk-and-350-expertsreveal ed-when-ai-will-overtake-humans.html.

Seatra, Henrik Skaug. "The Ghost in the Machine: Being Human in the Age of AI and Machine Learning." 2, vol. 1 (March 2019): 60-68. https://rd.springer.com/article/10.1007%2Fs42087-018-0039-1.

Sign of the End Time. "The Prophecy of Daniel 2." Accessed November 20, 2018. http://www.signs-of-end-times.com/daniel-2-prophecy.html.

Signorelli, Camilo Miguel. "Hypothesis and Theory Article: Can Computers Become Conscious and Overcome Humans?" Front. Robot AI. October 26, 2018. https://doi.org/10.3389/frobt.2018.00121.

Singer, Peter. *Ethics in the Real World: 82 Brief Essays on Things That Matter*, Princeton, NJ: Princeton University Press, 2016.

Smashingrobotic. "Thirteen Advanced Humanoid Robots for Sale Today." April 16, 2016. https://www.smashingrobotics.com/thirteen-advanced-humanoid-robots-for-sale-today.

Smith, Steward. "Military and Civilian Drone Use (UAV, UAS): The Future of Unmanned Aerial Vehicles." June 25, 2019. https://www.thebalancecareers.com/military-and-civilian-drone-use-4121099.

Sobol, Peter G. and Gary B. Ferngren, eds. *The History of Science and Religion in the Western Tradition, An Encyclopedia: Theories of the Soul.* New York, NY: Garland Publishing, 2000.

Spawforth, Tony. *The Story of Greece and Rome.* New Heaven and London: Yale University Press, 2018.

Statista.com. "Size of the Sex Toy Market Worldwide 2015-2020." Published August 9, 2019. https://www.statista.com/statistics/587109/size-of-the-global-sex-toy-market/.

Stone, Zara. "Everything You Need to Know about Sophia, the World's First Robot Citizen." *Forbes* (November 7, 2017). https://www.forbes.com/sites/zarastone/2017/11/07/everything-you-need-to-know-about-sophia-the-worlds-first-robotcitizen/#2dc18e9146fa.

StudyLight. "Bible Commentaries: Hawker's Poor Man's Commentary Daniel 2." Accessed October 25, 2019. https://www. studylight.org/commentaries/pmc/ daniel-2.html#37.

Stump J. B. and Alan G. Padgett. *The Blackwell Companion to Science and Christianity*, Malden, MA: Blackwell, 2012.

Sweet, Leonard. "Let Take a Walk." Napkin Scribbles Facebook Page. January 24, 2019. https://anchor.fm/napkinscribbles/episodes/Lets-Take-a-Walke2sakm?fbclid=IwA R3diKS58_ZXlYG2_lIyvTcSfq2S_Up6kDTwH9U mBt02VBRH5L_uItv0DA.

_____. *Nudge: Awakening Each Other to the God Who's Already There.* Colorado Spring, CO: David C. Cook, 2010.

_____. "Preach the Story." Facebook. February 27, 2020. https://www.facebook.com/PreachtheStory/posts/33 42547759094724?__tn__=-R.

Teich, Albert H. *Technology and the Future.* Boston, MA: Wadsworth Cengage Learning, 2009.

Templeton, John Marks, ed. *Evidence of Purpose: Scientists Discover the Creator.* New York, NY: Continuum, 1994.

Treacy, Siobhan. "Robot-Human Marriages: The Future of Marriage?" November 26, 2018. https://electronics360.globalspec.com/article/13207/robot-human-marriages-the-future-of-marriage.

Tweigye, Emanuel K. *Religion and Ethics for A New Age: Evolutionist Approach*. Lanham, MD: University Press of America, 2001.

Turing, A.M. "Computing Machinery and Intelligence." *Mind* 49:433-460. Accessed April 14, 2019. https://www.csee.umbc.edu/courses/471/papers/turing.pdf.

Vincent, James. "Putin Says the Nations That Leads in AI 'Will Be the Ruler of the World'." Accessed December 10, 2018. https://www.theverge.com/2017/9/4/16251226/russia-ai-putin-rule-the-world.

Vu, Michele A. "Survey: 1 in 3 Scientists Believe in God," July 16, 2009. https://www.christianpost.com/news/survey-one-third-of-scientists-believe-in-god.html.

Waldron, Jeremy. *One Another's Equals: The Basis of Human Equality*. Cambridge, MA: The Belknap Press of Harvard University, 2017.

Walvoord, John F. *Daniel: The Key to Prophetic Revelation*. Chicago, IL: Moody Press, 1971.

Warwick, Kevin. *Artificial: The Basic.* New York, NY: Routledge, 2012.

_____. *I, Cyborg.* Urbana, IL: University of Illinois, 2014.

Webb, Amy. *The Big Nine: How the Tech Titans and Their Thinking Machines Could Warp Humanity.* New York, NY: Public Affairs, 2019.

Whitcomb, John C. Jr. *Darius the Mede: A Study in History Identification.* Grand Rapids, MI: Eerdmans, 1959.

Wikipedia.com. "Alloy." Accessed November 30, 2019. https://en.wikipedia.org/wiki/Alloy.

_____. "Monkeys and Apes in Space." Accessed November 2, 2019. https://en.wikipedia.org/wiki/Monkeys_and_apes_i n_space.

_____. "Sophia (robot)." Accessed September 20, 2018. https://en.wikipedia.org/wiki/Sophia_(robot).

Yonck, Richard. *Heart of the Machine: Our Future in a World of Artificial Emotional Intelligence.* New York, NY: Arcade Publishing, 2017.

Young Edward J. *The Prophesy of Daniel.* Philadelphia, PA: W.B. Eerdmans Publishing, 1949.

Zarkadakis, George. *In Our Image: Savior or Destroyer? The History and Future of Artificial Intelligence.* New York, NY: Pegasus Books, 2016.

9 781662 833854